WAKE UP!

42 Ways to Improve Black America NOW!

❖❖❖❖❖❖

Gary A. McAbee

WAKE UP!

42 Ways to Improve Black America NOW!

❖❖❖❖❖❖

WAKE UP! 42 Ways to Improve Black America NOW!

Dedication
❖ ❖ ❖ ❖ ❖ ❖ ❖

This book is dedicated to so many people who have touched my life; without their love and support, nothing that I have accomplished would have been possible or worthwhile.

To my wife Belinda: thank you for standing by my side for better or worse, for richer or poorer, and in sickness and in health. Lord knows we've seen them all. Thank you for letting me know at the wedding ceremony that you would not "obey" my commands. It made me realize that you were a fighter who would be able to handle the good times and the bad times. Let the good times roll.

To our children Monique, Marquis, and Masai: you are the most beautiful children and a blessing to me. You will always be my greatest accomplishments and the greatest additions to my life.

To our parents: you have all been great examples of knowledge and wisdom, courage and strength. Now sit back, relax, and let us take care of you. Enjoy your grandchildren and continue to be a blessing in our lives. To my brothers and sisters: Jeffrey, Patrenia, Anessa, Joel, Tessie and your families, this is for you too.

To my church family: you are a collection of the greatest people I have ever met. You are all beautiful, respectful, supportive, God-loving people. You have added more to my, and my family's, lives than you realize. I love and cherish you all. We are going to make it just like Bishop Randall says every Sunday morning.

To my friends both old and new: you didn't see this coming did you? Malik, Tyrone, Larry "Skeet", Una, Bridgette, Shaherah, Yolanda, Brian,

Dedication

Genene, Valencia, Eddie, Jevon, Milton, Lawrence, Eric, Morris, Kyle, Bubby, Bruce, Ron, Peggy, Leroy "Tree", Alan, Russell, Kenny, and Diane.

To my current and former students: I hope that you continue to learn and apply the concepts I have taught you. Like I have said so many times, I expect to see you happy, healthy, and successful when we meet again in the future.

To all of the African American leaders and pioneers: you have influenced my dreams and goals in so many ways. You have been an inspiration to us all and your work will never be forgotten. You are all priceless treasures to our race, and to our world. We all owe you a sincere thank you and endless appreciation for all you have done.

To my African American family: we have been down for long enough. We have the potential and capability to do any and everything that we want to accomplish. We are a strong, enduring, and loving race of people. One day soon we will take our rightful place in our world.

To my human family: regardless of race, color, gender, or religious background, there are enough resources and opportunities for all us to grow and prosper. We are all in this together; all connected by our Creator in His divine plan. May we all find our way together and live in friendship, fellowship, and peace.

WAKE UP! 42 Ways to Improve Black America NOW!

Contents
❖ ❖ ❖ ❖ ❖ ❖

The First Word   8

Keys   12

Our Story   16

Education   37

Self-Motivation   58

Self-Improvement   84

Communication   107

Support   129

The Final Word   152

WAKE UP!

❖❖❖❖❖❖

WAKE UP! 42 Ways to Improve Black America NOW!

The First Word
❖ ❖ ❖ ❖ ❖ ❖

Thank God that Barack Obama became the 44th President of the United States on January 20, 2009, nearly 15 months before the publication of this book. Why did I wait for this long after such a monumental achievement to put out this book? It is because I knew that things would not change overnight, even though we elected an African-American President. I am still a tired and heartbroken, yet hopeful African-American man.

I am tired of the way that we, as a race, live our lives on a daily basis. I am still heartbroken because it seems like many things have gotten worse in my lifetime. We, in spite of all of the advantages this country has to offer, still come up short far too often. Our people are still caught in and endless cycle of violence, broken families, and self-destruction. Our communities are still in crisis and the future for too many black Americans looks bleak.

As I stared out of my window in my old neighborhood, I saw a huge vacant lot, overrun with weeds and garbage. This lot sat in the middle of a black inner-city neighborhood. The amount of empty liquor bottles was endless, not to mention the empty beer cans strewn across the lot. This lot was supposed to be a housing complex, a part of a neighborhood revitalization project from over ten years ago! Now it is another example of urban decay.

If this piece of property was in a middle class or affluent neighborhood, would it be used as a garbage dump, or would it be used properly? A lot like this does not exist in more affluent communities. Either it would be cleaned up or developed. It would not be left in this state of disrepair. The residents would not sit by and let it happen, let alone contribute to its decay.

The First Word

So what's the difference between my community and an affluent community? The obvious answer is the economic outlook of the communities and their people: some people choose to live in poverty-stricken neighborhoods and do little or nothing about it. Far too often, it is African Americans who find themselves in this position.

If you are tired and heartbroken by this, or other ills that plague African Americans, then this book is for you! It is also for all people, because the information on the following pages, though tailored to a black audience, is universal, and can be used by all people. It is about changing the mindset and thought processes of people. Better thoughts will result in better decisions.

I have directed this book's content at the African American community, since it is reflective of my heritage. Let's face facts: as a race, some of our thought processes are off base. The real issue is why the black community views itself the way it does. Why do we act as if we have so much self-hatred? Our self-hatred is so strong it clouds our judgment, our will, our decisions, our goals, our families, our relationships, and therefore, our entire lives. Unfortunately, not enough black Americans have learned how to "pull themselves up by the bootstraps" to rid themselves of self-hatred.

In order to pull ourselves up, we must realize the importance of educating our children. Uneducated children will struggle to find good employment. Without a good job, our children will struggle for most, if not all, of their lives. They will struggle to pay health insurance. They will struggle to afford housing in a safe community. They will struggle to stay out of debt. They will struggle to buy daily necessities. They will struggle to pay for quality education for their children. They will struggle to survive as adults. We must prevent this vicious cycle of struggle from becoming our children's legacy.

It's a good thing that we have some fighters in our community. Black people across the nation realize that we can change things; we can make a difference. They, like me, have not and will not give up. They come

WAKE UP! 42 Ways to Improve Black America NOW!

from all walks of life. They are living proof that black people can accomplish any and everything any American can. The American dream applies to us too, and we have numerous shining examples to prove it. These examples are there for us to study and recreate in order to become successful in this society.

I firmly believe that the only way to raise the fortunes of black people in America is for each black person in America to take personal responsibility for their own lives. Then, each black person can, in turn, help each other to raise their families and change our society. Being realistic, this ideal situation is a long way off, given the current state of black America. Yet, this book, like many other projects, is a starting point. Many of our greatest achievers all arrived at this point when attempting to influence change and make a difference.

Making a difference will require that we all pitch in. We should know the problems; now we must find some solutions. Real solutions can help every black American fix their own problems, which in turn will strengthen our families. Stronger families will lead to stronger communities. Stronger communities will lead to a stronger society. This is a movement that is long overdue.

At the core of this movement, the actions of each individual are most important. If only everyone would keep up their end of this bargain. We all must understand that we are all collectively in this together. The progress that I make has an effect on every black American if viewed in the proper context. Success breeds other successes, if the blueprint is followed carefully.

What is this blueprint? The blueprint is a series of ideas that can be used to live the life that we all are seeking. Regardless of our race, gender, origins, or economic status, we can all use the principles in this book to be more successful. This information is directed at African-Americans, the race that I belong to and feel has the most to gain from a collection like this. This book is not exclusively FUBU (For Us By Us, in case you didn't know); rather, it is FABM (For All By Me).

The First Word

I hope that everyone who reads this book takes in all of its principles with an open mind. I don't expect everyone to blindly follow my advice. In fact, I want my readers to question and challenge the information contained on the following pages. Some will find information they do not agree with. Others will use trial and error methods to find out what information works in their situation and apply it when necessary. Others will try some of the suggestions immediately. I believe that simply reading this book and becoming more knowledgeable is a wonderful start. Anyone whose life is improved because of reading this book is a blessing.

I am confident that these principles will work. The question is whether or not we will get more of our people to use them. The highest achievers in our race have discovered many of these concepts long before the thought crossed my mind to write this book. Believe that their success can be duplicated; reading this book is a start. Best wishes and blessings on your journey through the following thoughts and ideas. I sincerely hope that the words that follow will inspire us all to improve our lives and fix Black America NOW!

WAKE UP! 42 Ways to Improve Black America NOW!

Keys
❖ ❖ ❖ ❖ ❖ ❖

There are six categories in the first of two volumes that cover a wide range of topics that we can use to fix black America now. Each of these concepts is a key principle that we can use. The foundation that we must build upon is to learn who we are as a race. Throughout OUR HISTORY both here and abroad, we have been survivors, builders, and high achievers. Once we learn these truths, we need to understand that each one of us has a stake in the success and uplifting of our race, and we can duplicate past successes.

After that, the first practical application we need to put into practice is improving our EDUCATION; particularly, our children's education. Education to the key; knowledge is power. When teaching, this was my message everyday without exception. It should be the same message that is delivered in every African- American household. Once we build our knowledge base, we must become SELF MOTIVATED to use what we learn to get what we want.

After becoming motivated, SELF IMPROVEMENT is the next logical step. By looking inward, we can work on ourselves, then guide and mentor others. This can be accomplished through effective COMMUNICATION. Communication skills allow us to provide SUPPORT to our African- American brothers and sisters.

In volume two, the next six keys we be introduced to complete our journey. We need to learn LESSONS in life that we can build upon. One of the things that we should do to support each other is talk about issues like improving the lives of each and every FAMILY in our communities.

Another important step is to branch out and discover things that we do not see enough, such as maintaining our FINANCES. Getting our financial houses in order is a way to fix many of the ills that plague our lives. We can improve our finances through rendering quality

Keys

SERVICES to each other. These services should first be offered to our people in our COMMUNITIES to help rebuild our infrastructure. Building stronger communities will allow us to compete, contribute, and take our rightful place in SOCIETY.

When we learn how to use each of these key principles, we will be able to improve our lives immediately.

WAKE UP! 42 Ways to Improve Black America NOW!

OUR STORY
❖

1. Accept the Fact That Black is Beautiful
2. Learn the History of Africa
3. Remember Slavery in America
4. Remember Jim Crow to Segregation
5. Remember the Civil Rights Movement
6. Learn About Your Family Tree
7. Learn the Stories of Successful Black People

EDUCATION
❖❖

8. Turn off the Television
9. Read
10. Stress the importance of education
11. Be active in your child's education
12. Think about Higher Education
13. Do Your Homework
14. Learn About Your Health and Well Being

SELF-MOTIVATION
❖❖❖

15. Believe in a Higher Power
16. Find the Right Church Home
17. Keep the Faith
18. Use Four Natural Laws
19. Follow Your Senses
20. Positive Mental Outlook
21. Be Enthusiastic

Keys

SELF-IMPROVEMENT
❖❖❖❖

22. You Might as Well Excel
23. Develop and Use the IT Factor
24. Starve Yourself to Get Hungry
25. Write Down Your Goals/Set Time Limits
26. Control Your Destiny/Stay the Course
27. Accept Your Results
28. Keep Your Word/Honor Your Commitments

COMMUNICATION
❖❖❖❖❖

29. Master the Written and Spoken English Language
30. Learn the Power of Words: Quotes
31. Learn a Second Language
32. You Are a Reflection of Your Race
33. Improve Your Body Language
34. Dress for Success
35. Stop Promoting Anger

SUPPORT
❖❖❖❖❖❖

36. Be a Stereotype Breaker
37. Avoid Spreading Negative Energy
38. Don't be a Dream Stealer
39. Give Advice Under Two Conditions
40. Don't Mess With My Code of Ethics
41. Choose a Positive Role Model
42. Surround Yourself With Positive People

WAKE UP! 42 Ways to Improve Black America NOW!

OUR STORY: A KEY TO WAKING UP BLACK AMERICA!
❖

By learning Our Story, we can wake up people in our race who lack the ability to overcome their current problems just by showing them who they are. For hundreds of years, black people worldwide have been systematically led to believe that we are an inferior race of people. Nothing could be farther from the truth; so many attempts have been made to convince us of our inferiority.

African Americans should be proud of our heritage as builders, inventors, and creators. We have survived, from our ancestors who lived in Africa, to our present day high achieving black Americans. We are a strong race of people who will never be destroyed or defeated. The proof is in our story of enduring greatness.

1. The Truth Is: Black is Still Beautiful!
2. Learn Our Story in Africa: We Are Worthy
3. Remember Slavery in America: We Are Survivors
4. Remember Jim Crow to Segregation: We Are Brave
5. Remember the Civil Rights Movement: We Are Conquerors
6. Learn About Your Family Tree: We Are Valuable
7. Learn the Stories of Successful Black People: We Are Successful

Respect Our Story

Our Story

#1 The Truth is: Black is Still Beautiful!

Throughout the Civil Rights era, something great was rediscovered. We remembered that we are a beautiful race of people, on the inside as well as our outward appearances. Black Nationalism, a belief that blacks in America should take pride in our race, took shape. The sayings were numerous, from "I'm black and I'm proud" to "black is beautiful". These sayings helped to establish pride in our communities and lift our collective spirits. African Americans finally realized that we are a beautiful race of people.

Sometimes it seems that adversity brings about change, so it is easy to see why the adversities faced during the Civil Rights Era would spawn a movement of Black pride. Using that logic, one should conclude that today's troubling times would be right to cultivate a new movement of black pride. However, universally this is not the case. We are making progress, but the progress we make seems to be in small circles. A challenge from an outside force that we all can clearly see is the only way we will get the masses of African Americans back to believing in black pride, and believing that we are still a beautiful race of people.

Right now, we are too separated; we are not united by a singular cause. Although many issues stand out such as crime, the lack of quality education, or single-parent families, we are still in need of a rallying point. We need a lightning rod to unite us, then our pride, determination, and beauty would rise once again. The main reason why this has not happened since the Civil Rights Era is our comfort level in this country. We, as a race, are comfortable where we are today. Therefore we make a huge mistake when we allow the wrong things to show the world our beauty and black pride.

We show our pride in materialistic things. Our children have cell phones, I-pods, and video game systems. They are comfortable. Our adults drive nice cars, wear expensive clothes, and buy fancy jewelry. They are comfortable. These things make us look and feel "beautiful!" Yet far too

WAKE UP! 42 Ways to Improve Black America NOW!

often, we neglect to see the negative things happening in our households, families, and communities that take away from our beauty. The negative things we have yet to overcome are a direct result of years of being comfortable.

Black America, you are too comfortable! You are resigned to the "fact" that our problems are either too widespread, or too far gone, to understand that we need a dose of our beautiful black pride. We need to get back to our roots, and to learn how our ancestors managed to persevere through situations far more difficult than we face today. We need to learn that the beauty in our race starts from within, from our spirit and strength that can not be destroyed.

Our spirits have been bruised, tortured, and scarred, but we as a people have always moved forward. The only explanation for this is our beauty. The same beauty that existed 1,000 years ago in the kingdoms of Africa still exists today. The same beauty that helped our ancestors survive in slave ships while being transported across the ocean to foreign lands still exists today. The same beauty that kept us while we were in shackles through years of hard labor still exists today. The same beauty that endured public segregation and humiliation still exists today. The same beauty that faced the injustice of discrimination still exists today.

Our beauty is:

Rosa Parks sitting in her bus seat in quiet defiance of an unjust law...

Michael Jordan going up for his last, championship winning jump shot...

Harriet Tubman leading slaves through dark swamps on the way to freedom...

Nelson Mandela dancing to celebrate his victory over years of false imprisonment...

Our Story

Condoleeza Rice meeting with heads of state to discuss issues of global interest...

Martin Luther King Jr. delivering a speech that stirs the soul of his audience forever...

The wonderful thing about this is that each of us, as black Americans, have this beautiful power in ourselves, and in our families. It is there, waiting for us to discover it, explore it, and embrace it. Beauty is ours! A key to waking up Black America is to examine "Our Story" to help us find solutions to our problems. We must accept the fact that Black is, was, and always will be, BEAUTIFUL!

WAKE UP BLACK AMERICA! Being black is still beautiful!

WAKE UP! 42 Ways to Improve Black America NOW!

#2 Learn Our Story of Our Origins in Africa: We Are Worthy!

Our story begins in Africa, thousands of years ago. If we review what we have seen and heard about Africa, many things should come to mind. We all know that the first man was an African from 2 million years ago. We know that Egyptians were one of the wealthiest and powerful civilizations in world history. We also know of the images you see about poor Africans who are undernourished and impoverished. However, we need to know more, a lot more.

We can not be deterred by those who want African Americans to return to our homeland. This thought process is faulty, mainly because those who make this claim do not understand the rich heritage of the African continent. They do not read about the history of Africa nor its people. They do not examine the pictures that illustrate the beauty of the continent. They do not plan to visit and see for themselves. The most unfortunate part of this is that we, as African Americans, do not experience any of these things either.

It is amazing that so many people, including African Americans, are not aware of the history of the Motherland. The images we see of past and present Africa would lead us to believe that the continent is little more than a wasteland. However, nothing is farther from the truth. Historically, if we examine the past we will come to understand that Africa was once one of the richest continents of the world.

People from around the globe traded with ancient Africans, making Africa a wealthy continent. In each region of Africa, different commodities brought wealth. Gold, silver, diamonds, and animal skins were commodities that were traded worldwide. This brought huge profits to traders, who spurred the growth of cities and centers of trade. The African civilizations flourished for thousands of years, long before colonization and slavery was introduced to the continent.

Our Story

The following information is a brief listing of the peoples, kingdoms, and commodities that made each geographic region of Africa an important area. After reading this section, we should all do our research and find out more about our African roots. The history of Africa is far too large to cover here, yet it is important for us, as African Americans, to know that if our ancestors enjoyed success on the world stage, so can we. Maybe this will inspire us to do the same.

In Northeast Africa:

-Kingdom of Nubia existed 10,000 years ago
-Kingdom of Kush existed 4,000 years ago
-both societies were advanced in science and mathematics
-trading copper, silver, and ivory worldwide generated wealth

In Southern Africa:

-Kingdom of Zimbabwe traded with China 800 years ago
-houses were made of stone and bricks
-gold trading and metal works were the center of industry
-cities of 15,000 people were some of the largest in the world

In Eastern Africa:

-Swahili civilization was known for its great warriors
-trade of gold, ivory, and leopard skins created immense wealth
-trade partnerships with Japan, China, and Korea
-Zanzibar became a major center of trade

In Western Africa:

-Kingdom of Ghana existed 1,300 years ago
-Kingdom of Mali existed 1,000 years ago
-gold and copper were traded for salt
-Timbuktu had one of the earliest modern universities 700 years ago

WAKE UP! 42 Ways to Improve Black America NOW!

Each of the events listed lead us to an important point in our story: when our ancestors were enslaved and brought to North America. Africans gave us a rich history to build upon, and our ancestors held up their end of the bargain. For in slavery, we should appreciate our ability to survive and overcome.

WAKE UP BLACK AMERICA! Learn about our origins in Africa!

#3 Remember Our Story of Slavery in America: We Are Survivors!

Slavery is still a taboo subject in the history of the United States. It's like having a pink elephant in the room that everyone can clearly see but no one wants to talk about. The history books gloss over the topic of slavery; therefore, making it seem less destructive to our race then and now. It really is still destructive because its scars are still felt by us as a people today. The scars this trail has left behind can be traced from the first slaves who arrived in America in 1619 to African Americans today. This is why we must learn about the slavery period, remember its effects, and celebrate our survival.

Celebration is the perfect word for the issue of slavery. We should celebrate our survival of the period of slavery, not lament about it. We should take pride all of the accomplishments of our ancestors who survived against impossible odds. If we look at it this way, we will come to understand that our ancestors survived for us. Without their determination, we would not be able to have the advantages we have in today's America.

To celebrate the slavery period, we must first remember the people, places, and events that shaped OUR STORY. Slavery is a story of facing adversity, huge odds, and overwhelming disadvantages to become a part of American society. It should be looked at and reflected upon for the struggles and our ancestor's ability to overcome their hardships.

We could do this by putting ourselves in their place by using a lot of imagination. We should also avoid injecting our own, modern belief system into the story. For example, some people today say if they faced slavery, they would have fought their way out. It wouldn't have happened. So when we examine slavery by using our imagination, we can learn to appreciate those who lived though it. Think about it. How would you have handled...

WAKE UP! 42 Ways to Improve Black America NOW!

...forcefully being taken away from your community?

...permanently being separated from your family?

...unwillingly being transported to a land over 1,000 miles away?

...living on a ship with hundreds of others in limited space and subhuman conditions?

...not being able to figure out where you were when you arrived?

...being sold to a stranger and forced to live with strangers?

...being forced to work without wages in poor living conditions for your entire life?

...watching your children born into the same lifestyle of slavery?

...growing older until dying as a slave without gaining freedom?

If we were able to analyze each of those statements and honestly assess the situation, most would say they would have done something. But what could have been done? What could they have done? Resistance often led to death or harder burdens. Instead, most of the slaves endured their hardship and lived their lives in a quiet, yet determined way to survive. They hoped for, dreamed of, and prayed about a way to survive and gain their freedom. This example is perfect for us in today's society: hope, dream, pray, SURVIVE.

This is why we can learn lessons from slavery. Reading the stories of personal triumphs during the slavery period reveals to us that any obstacle or any problem can be overcome. If our ancestors could do it in far worse conditions than we face today, then there is no excuse why we can not do the same thing now. We can look at the life of James Forten, who became one of the most respected African Americans thanks to his sailing experiences during the slavery period. We can look at the life of

Our Story

Harriet Tubman, who took immediate action to improve her life and the lives of others. These are our role models, people from our past who can unlock the secrets of survival.

So slavery can help us if we accept it, embrace its legacy, and reexamine it. It is a key to help us today. It should be celebrated because it is the story of survival. We should research it ourselves, because our school systems do not put slavery in this proper context. Remember, it is still taboo to over-examine this in the classroom. We should tell our children about it so they know that overcoming long odds is a part of the African American experience. We should be proud of our ancestors and link ourselves to their legacy.

WAKE UP BLACK AMERICA! We are survivors!

WAKE UP! 42 Ways to Improve Black America NOW!

#4 Remember Our Story of Jim Crow to Segregation: We Are Brave!

One of the biggest myths in our history is the role Abraham Lincoln played in freeing our slave ancestors. At first, Lincoln would have allowed slavery to continue in the South if the Southern states would have agreed to stay in the United States! This means that his first intentions were not to free and uplift black Americans! Continuing forward, after freeing the slaves, Lincoln put in his agenda to help uplift the former slaves. Unfortunately, he was assassinated before he could do his work. Lincoln's death left former slaves without the help they needed to start their lives after slavery.

So once again, our ancestors faced another challenge: a threat to their survival. They could find little help from the government. At this point, black Americans showed how brave they really were. Former slaves worked side by side with former slave owners to farm the land as sharecroppers. They adapted and learned how to move forward. Others moved north to connect with black Americans who already lived there. They reunited with families and started new lives.

These were bold steps to take for thousands of newly freed slaves. It took a lot of bravery because their assimilation into American society was not quick or easy. Jim Crow laws that limited the rights of black Americans spread across the South. It was the new form of slavery and it would last for 80 years. These laws covered everything from voting rights to land ownership and beyond. Black Americans struggled to find their way, so their bravery in the midst of their struggles had to be a part of their daily lives.

Meanwhile, in northern cities blacks found it difficult to find jobs and adequate housing. Overcrowding was a result of the shift of blacks to places like Chicago, Detroit, and Cleveland. The great migration is the reason why many black Americans find themselves in northern cities and

Our Story

towns today. As a result, as more blacks moved in, a subtle wave of discrimination soon followed.

So blacks had difficult struggles while trying to become true American citizens. Pioneers like Booker T. Washington and W.E.B. DuBois helped and left lasting legacies by providing inspiration to black Americans. They both encouraged blacks to raise their standing as Americans. They both realized that we would eventually gain our rightful place in society, but only after the proper groundwork was laid.

Other black Americans also made significant contributions during this time period. How many African Americans know who A.G. Gaston was? If we do our research, we would find out that he was one of the greatest entrepreneurs, black or white, in US history. We could also learn about Madame CJ Walker, who is credited with being the first black millionaire AND the first female millionaire. We can not forget the contributions of Elijah McCoy, who was a famous inventor. Although disputed, there are accounts that attribute a famous saying to this one of a kind inventor. Have you ever used the phrase, "the real mccoy?"

All of these famous black Americans and countless others moved through the Jim Crow era and made enough progress to lead to the more radical concept of limiting rights of blacks called segregation. The Declaration of Independence, written over 100 years earlier, stated that all men are created equal. Segregation was a backhanded attempt to implement this concept because it discriminated by providing "separate but equal" services and facilities. Of course, the facilities were rarely the same.

The African American who we should remember for his accomplishments during this time period was Supreme Court Justice Thurgood Marshall. Without his contributions, there is little doubt that we would not be where we are as a race today. His most celebrated achievement was the invalidation of the concept "separate but equal," thanks to the landmark Brown vs. Board of Education case. Justice

WAKE UP! 42 Ways to Improve Black America NOW!

Marshall saw the inequality that blacks faced, and was at the forefront of ending this unjust practice.

Once again we should use our imagination to step into this situation to prove the greatness of our ancestors. Imagine being forced to use separate, less than adequate water fountains, bathrooms, and public entrances. Imagine not being able to sit in the front section of a bus or being herded into a train car for blacks only. Imagine being prevented from staying at a local hotel; or being able to sit and eat at a local restaurant. All of these things created a period of adjustment, resentment, and mobilization for blacks.

We can take away a lot from these experiences. It proves the old saying, "when the going gets tough, the tough get going". Blacks eventually got going. They did something about their plight. They chose to fight back by using methods that were not illegal; instead, they followed the laws of the land. In other words, they became creative to find solutions to their problems, just like we can learn how to be creative to solve our problems today. We can learn valuable lessons from our heroic ancestors.

WAKE UP BLACK AMERICA! We are brave!

Our Story

#5 Remember Our Story of the Civil Rights Movement: We are conquerors!

During the Civil Rights Movement, African Americans took action. At no point in our history were we more active and united. Our race fought battle after battle and endured hardship after hardship to secure the rights they should have already earned as American citizens. Instead, once again, they were treated as outsiders who had to take action to finally become full fledged Americans.

The first thing we should remember is that the chapter in our story about the Civil Rights Movement is a recent struggle. In terms of history, this is something that happened only 50 years ago. This means that it was only one or two generations ago; many of our parents lived through the struggle. They witnessed first hand, watched on television, or read in newspapers about the progress of the movement. As survivors of the period, the previous generation represents living history. Their knowledge is a treasure. It was, and still is, their responsibility to enlighten and inspire future generations with the freedoms won during this time.

Another aspect of this time period we should understand is the impact that we had on the world stage. Our struggle has always been watched by the entire world. We were the true example of the processes of democracy at work. We proved that the system of democracy works, even when some don't want it to equally function for all people. We protested as a part of our right to assemble; we spoke out as a part of our right of free speech; we petitioned the government as a part of our right of due process. Democracy was being tested and put on trial by black Americans, and thank GOD that it lived up to its lofty ideals.

A third viewpoint of the Civil Rights Era is the magnitude of its place in American history, not only for blacks, but for the entire country. The turbulent years of the 50s and 60s have been called a turning point for

WAKE UP! 42 Ways to Improve Black America NOW!

black America. We were at a serious crossroads. We could have been forced to take a step back in time, definitely not into slavery, but probably into more discrimination and segregation. This would have been a struggle our generation would be involved in today. Instead, we gained our rightful place in American society. Our lifestyle is a direct result of the Civil Rights Movement. We should be thankful.

Here are some other things about the Civil Rights Era that black Americans should be thankful for:

-President John F. Kennedy was a hero to most black Americans, but Lyndon Johnson pushed through his Civil rights agenda after his death. History tells us that Johnson staked his Presidency on improving society and Civil Rights, not fighting the Vietnam War. His legacy should also be celebrated by black Americans. Thank you.

-Rosa Parks was tired so she just wanted to sit down! It wasn't her intention to start a movement, yet her refusal to give up her seat was the spark that set the Civil Rights Movement in motion. We should remember that her act of defiance was born out of the courage to silently declare that enough is enough. Thank you.

-Parts of our country were more dangerous for black Americans than being in our nation's wars. Our blood was shed on the back roads of Mississippi, on fields in Georgia, and across bridges in Alabama. Many people of the era gave their lives so we could be free today. Thank you.

-Dr. King is the greatest leader of the Civil Rights Era, but he was certainly not alone. Malcolm X, Medgar Evers, James Meredith, Stokely Carmichael, Fannie Lou Hamer, Andrew Young, and countless others also led the charge. It was their leadership that helped black America move forward to see a brighter day. Thank you.

Finally, we need to appreciate the fact that most of the institutions that closed their doors to African Americans were finally integrated. We seem to take it for granted that we were always able to move about the

Our Story

country freely, attend the schools of our choice, or ride wherever we wanted to on public transportation. The Civil Rights movement changed all of this. We should never forget that this was only 50 years ago. In my opinion, we should celebrate this period more, just because of the strides we made as a race.

The Civil Rights Movement brought out the true strength and pride of the black race. It's the kind of effort we need in the 21st century to reverse the fortunes of thousands of black Americans. First of all, we need to understand that everything we have today is because of the Civil Rights Era. Without this effort, we would still be constantly fighting against a wave of discrimination and segregation. Secondly, this effort takes leadership; the kind of leadership offered by Martin Luther King Jr., Malcolm X, and others. We need this kind of leadership to wake up black America today.

WAKE UP BLACK AMERICA! We are conquerors!

#6 Learn About Your Family Tree: We Are Valuable!

Another important aspect that African Americans can not allow to go unmentioned is learning about our personal histories. Each African American has a connection to ancestors who were survivors, creators, and builders. In all of our families, our ancestors fit this description. Therefore, we can all benefit from learning about our families and our family tree. Indeed we have a rich heritage in the history of our country.

The one thing that I regret the most in life is not learning more about one segment of my family from my grandmother. Grand mom Frasier, God rest her soul, was a great source of information for our family. Although she was advanced in age and I was young, she gave me insights into her past. I listened to her intently because of her obvious wealth of knowledge. My problem was that I wasn't old enough to appreciate her stories.

She told me about a time when she and my grandfather were driving in a car in the South. They were threatened and my grandfather had to protect her with his gun. I don't remember if he used that gun, but it sure was an interesting story. It showed me that blacks in the South had to be careful when traveling in those days. It also showed how courageous my grandfather was, and the fact that he would protect his family at all costs. It is a lesson that is not lost; not necessarily the need to pull a gun, but the need to be a strong husband, father, and provider for my family.

Another fascinating example in my family is on my father's side. The McAbee family has its roots in Damascus, Maryland. My family there lived in a log house; in fact, the house still stands today. Yes, it is still in the McAbee family. It is registered as a historic site in its county, and in the state of Maryland. Surrounded by corn fields, it's a place where we used to play as children long before we realized its local significance. This house is a source of pride for everyone who has lived in it as well as those who have visited the McAbee family of Damascus, Maryland.

Our Story

Our history also shows the migration patterns of our relatives. After being born in the South, all of my grandparents moved north to pursue better opportunities. The same can be said for many black people. However, the roots left behind in the South are well established. My family still has a major presence in South Carolina, while being spread out throughout Northern states as well. This is a trait few other races of people in the United States can claim.

How can we follow the migration patterns and characteristics of our families? We can start by creating a family tree. My family tree is filled with stories. Not all of them are good stories. Some of my family members had various illnesses and mental health issues. Others were workers at various jobs for long periods of time. Each of these people has a story to tell, a life that is tied to mine. All of these people make me proud of their accomplishments and proud to be an African American.

My father has a picture of our family tree that traces our lineage all the way back to Africa and the unknown slave who is the founder of our family. Some of the details still need to be filled in, but the groundwork has been laid. When I first saw the tree, I had many questions about the people on its branches. I could remember meeting some of these people as a child. They left behind many unanswered questions; questions that I will have answered some day. It's sad that we don't know more about our family members and the legacies they left behind.

In my opinion, the most important question that can not be answered is the gap between the African and his slave ancestor who was brought to America. Although most people can not trace their roots all the way back to Africa, we can learn about our history as a race in America. This will allow us to WAKE UP, and realize that we can overcome all obstacles, hardships, and challenges that we face in the same ways that others in our families have been able to do.

WAKE UP BLACK AMERICA! Learn about your family tree!

WAKE UP! 42 Ways to Improve Black America NOW!

#7 Learn Our Story of Successful Black People: We Are Successful!

Thanks to the advances we have made from slavery to the Civil Rights Era; we have been left a remarkable gift by the highest achievers of our race. The gift is their stories of success. We all MUST learn about each of these successful people and many more if we are going to tap into ways that will lead to greatness. We need to understand that most, if not all, of the successful people in our race started with little or nothing. Yet, they were able to use what they had to achieve great things. If they could achieve success, why can't we, with all of the resources we have in the 21st century, become successful too?

We all know about Dr. Martin Luther King Jr. This is because he is one of the few African-American leaders we learn about in school. This is why there is an old joke that goes around about trying to answer a question about a successful black American. The "answer" is always Martin Luther King. Who was the first black American to run in a marathon? Don't know? Say Martin Luther King!

It is a funny joke, but not because it makes you laugh. It's funny because it is a true, yet very sad commentary on our knowledge of successful black people. We just don't know enough about black pioneers and creators. There are thousands of books that contain the "secrets" of our race. We have autobiographies of black Americans such as Booker T. Washington and Malcolm X. We have poetry, created by Phyllis Wheatley and Maya Angelou. We have the magazines produced by John Johnson and Earl Graves.

All of this means that finding and reading literature created by or written about successful black Americans should not be a problem. We have been active in the political arena. Our political leaders have scored countless victories that have not only benefited black Americans, but all races of people. We should be proud of their accomplishments and celebrate their successes. Shirley Chisholm and Maxine Waters are

Our Story

shining examples of the impact African-American women can have in politics. Douglas Wilder and Tom Bradley proved that black men could be elected and handle state and large city governments. They all proved to us that it can be done. We simply need to find out how they became successful and use their methods to duplicate their success.

In order to build upon the success of others, we must learn about them. Unfortunately, as a whole, African Americans don't read enough or do our own research unless we have to. We should be willing and able to learn about our true heroes: successful black Americans who paved the way for us today. The internet is a blessing to us because we can easily find all there is to know about successful African Americans. There is no excuse why we do not know about the highest achievers in our race.

So the readers of this book have an assignment: to learn more about the following African Americans. First, search for their biographies. What were their beginnings? Next, read about their achievements. What were their goals? What obstacles did they overcome? Finally, learn their secrets to emulate their successes. What achievements make them famous?

The following list of famous African Americans should be researched to learn more about their legacies and contributions to our race. It consists of African- American men and women who achieved greatness in various walks of life. Purposely, it does not include famous athletes or modern day entertainers. Although their contributions are very important, if asked, I am confident that most of them would attribute their success to people on this list. If not, then they have an assignment too!

Some Famous Black Americans

1. Fannie Lou Hamer
2. Paul Robeson
3. Marian Anderson
4. Mae Jemison

WAKE UP! 42 Ways to Improve Black America NOW!

5. Earl Graves
6. Booker T Washington
7. Benjamin Banneker
8. Madame CJ Walker
9. Ben Carson
10. Frederick Douglas
11. Thurgood Marshall
12. Shirley Chisholm
13. Phyllis Wheatley
14. Mary McLeod Bethune
15. Sojourner Truth
16. Matthew Henson
17. W.E. B. Dubois
18. Granville T. Woods
19. Frederick Douglass
20. Bessie Coleman

After learning about these outstanding examples of success, we should not let our research about the achievements of African Americans stop here. These are only 20 out of millions of successful black Americans worldwide. Our race has produced some of the brightest, most creative minds in human history. We can learn volumes from these people and put their action plans to work immediately. The question is: are we as a race ready, willing, and able to use our heroes as our role models so our race can become successful?

WAKE UP BLACK AMERICA! We are successful!

EDUCATION: A KEY TO FIXING BLACK AMERICA!
❖❖

Now that we have learned about our value as a race and our achievements, we can start the journey of applying knowledge to wake up black America. This process must begin with EDUCATION. There is an old cliché that says: Knowledge is Power. Without collectively expanding our knowledge base, African Americans as a race will always be one step behind when pursuing dreams and goals.

We all know the importance of education. Without a good education, black Americans are not able to take full advantage of the opportunities in our country. Our children must be taught this simple fact immediately. The days of lamenting school and building knowledge must come to an end TODAY. If not, then our lives will not be as fulfilling and our talents will not be fully realized. Therefore African Americans must understand the importance of education for us and our children…

8. Limit How Often You Watch Television
9. Read
10. Stress the Importance of Education
11. Be Active in Your Child's Education
12. Think About Higher Education
13. Do Your Homework
14. Learn About Your Health and Well Being

Respect Our Story-Build Knowledge Through Education

WAKE UP! 42 Ways to Improve Black America NOW!

#8 Limit How Often You Watch Television

We are in the new golden age of television. For black Americans, this golden age far too often portrays us in the worst possible light. As I turned on the television recently, what was the first thing I saw? A talk show had a topic about controlling, overbearing men who verbally, mentally, and physically abuse their women. Of course, the first two men on the show are black men. In fact, they are two of the worst possible examples of young African-American men you can find. Unfortunately, the perception many people outside our race have about us is often based on what they see on television.

On another "talk" show, we had paternity DNA testing. The young woman, no more than 18 years of age, swore up and down that she was 1000% sure he is the father of her baby. Meanwhile, a young black man waited in the wings. He was dressed as a "thug", with a rag on his head, and a gold tooth or two in his mouth. "There ain't no way in hell that's my baby!" He went on to call the young lady what seemed to be every foul name in the book, including bitch, ho, and slut. Her response: a mouthful of curses, anger, and defiance. "Bring his ass out here!" The crowd roars its approval of two young, lost African-American souls showing their true colors on national television.

He comes out, and throws what look like gang signs and middle fingers in the air. At this point, there are so many cuss words flying through the air that the soundboard operator had to be having a hard time beeping out all the profanity. Finally, after an award-winning performance, both people listen for the verdict. "You are….. not the father!!!" The young lady denies the result while the young man celebrates his victory. The crowd goes crazy. Meanwhile, another black child will suffer, caught in a vicious cycle of being born out of wedlock. I forgot to mention that this young lady had been on the show five times before, each time accusing a different man of being this child's father.

Education

I decided to move on, giving my trusted remote a workout until I found another great show. On this one, we follow local police departments in action, rounding up the bad guys. On this episode, the police spot two black men who had to be up to no good. Of course, they were. They were involved in a drug transaction, and the police gave chase. Naturally, the chase took the cameras through a maze of urban decay and blight. All around the housing project, black folks, both young and old, stood and watched as if this was an everyday occurrence.

When the police finally caught the suspect, they proceeded to question him. His English was so poor that I had to wonder what his level of education was. Of course, he possessed bags of crack rocks, a wad of cash, and a small knife. Another young black male arrested. He admitted to the officer that he had been arrested for drugs before. This undoubtedly would lead to jail time. He was escorted to a police car and taken to jail: a place where you can find more black men than there are on all college campuses. The officer closed the segment by explaining to the audience how the neighborhood works: young drug dealers who run rampant and terrorize the community to make their money.

Finally I switched gears and found another reason to cringe: a music video, at 11:25 AM, where kids could easy tune in to see sex, lies, and the degradation of our black women. The artist spewed lyrics that described his ability to "freak" women, drive the best cars, and get of trouble with the police. In a video and in some music, this is a lifestyle that we should be proud of. Well it is not. Maybe he was the father; maybe he could have helped that drug dealer avoid the cops too!

The images in the video were even worse. His look was "ghetto": baggy jeans, white tee, fitted baseball hat, sneakers, and a gold chain. Certainly, this could be a fitting role model for my sons. And there were role models for my daughter too. Many of them, scantily clad, were busy shaking body parts I didn't know existed. I'll admit that I enjoy the female anatomy, but this was too racy for television, especially so early in the day. Other images included champagne bottles, money, fancy cars, and of course, more half-naked women.

WAKE UP! 42 Ways to Improve Black America NOW!

In one half hour I witnessed several, destructive images of black people and harmful reflections of our community. Teen pregnancy, children born out of wedlock, fathers who will not take responsibility for their children all plague the structure of our family. Drug dealing, multiple arrests, and prisons filled with black men ruin the fabric of our communities. Harsh lyrics, foul language, and harmful images of women tear at the perception of how blacks in America should live.

It is also a problem when television defines who African Americans are to our own people. The reality television craze has made celebrities out of ordinary people who get 15 minutes of fame. For African Americans, many of these new role models gain a huge national following by being controversial, provocative, or downright stereotypical. Their success is not the issue; I am all for taking advantage of opportunities that exist. The issue is that they are not the best role models for us.

The point of this exercise is to be clear that there are few quality images of blacks on television. Even when there are a few, they are often vilified. Remember when Bill Cosby played Dr. Huxtable, and Phylicia Rashad played his lawyer wife on the Cosby Show for years. In our community, the show was often called unrealistic because they were educated, had good jobs, and made good money. They were viewed more as a "white" family because of their success. Some couldn't believe that black people could live like the Huxtables!

The solution to this problem is to turn off the television. At the least, we should limit the hours that we watch television to a minimum. The images we see become ingrained into our minds, our subconscious thoughts. Then they are manifested in actions we take, feelings we possess, attitudes towards others. This is especially true when dealing with people of other races, who may not come into contact enough with many black people. They might not realize that most of us are nothing like the destructive images they view on television.

WAKE UP BLACK AMERICA! Avoid watching too much television!

Education

#9 Read

The statistic is alarming: the average American reads one book per year! One book! How many people think that the statistic is actually lower for black Americans? Unfortunately, we do not read as much as we should. We have a wealth of books written on every subject imaginable, yet we do not take full advantage of reading. Reading develops many skills that can help us improve our lives. In turn, we can inspire our children to read more as well.

As a child, I had a habit of looking in my parent's encyclopedia set (remember the encyclopedia!) I used to look at everything, from biographies of famous people to countries. One thing that really stuck with me was map reading. I taught myself how to read maps of many countries of the world, especially the United States. If something interested me, I would also read about each place on the map. When we would travel, I would remember places I saw and read about. Now I can read maps flawlessly, easily finding places on the fly and providing directions to places I rarely visit. This can be attributed to reading at an early age.

By now you should know Dr. Ben Carson! He chronicled his illustrious career in his book, *Think Big*. In the book he described his struggles academically as a child. He was considered retarded by teachers, administrators, and other children. When did he change, and suddenly ascend to the top of his class? It happened because his mother made him and his brother read two books per week! They also had to write a report on each book.

Now let's do some quick math:

    2 books per week
X 52 weeks
=104 books per year

WAKE UP! 42 Ways to Improve Black America NOW!

When Dr. Carson read 104 books per year, his classmates didn't. He improved his grades across the board: from mathematics, to language arts, to spelling, and of course, reading. He also learned a lot about his favorite subject, science. It was this knowledge that led him to become one of the top students in his class, and paved the way for him to become of the greatest surgeons in history.

Just like Ben Carson's mother, our challenge is to get our children to want to read more. One way is to have parents lead the way by reading themselves. Children are likely to model the behavior of their parents, so parents should also set an example by reading to their children. Additionally, children should have a period of time that is devoted to reading outside of school.

A great way to incorporate reading into our children's lives is to go to the library. As a child, two of my biggest thrills were my first library card and the monthly arrival of the bookmobile at my school. By today's standards, this may sound far fetched, but things have not changed that much. Children love to read, but they tend to stop reading when things like the television, video games, and music present themselves as "better" options. Therefore, a parent should limit these opportunities and promote reading instead.

Children are not the only ones to benefit from reading. Adults can too. As African Americans, we have a wealth of literature written by black authors to read. Most bookstores now have a complete section of African American literature. Indeed, we have written books on various subjects. Each one of these books gives clues on how to improve ourselves through reading. We also have African-American bookstores where we can find a much better selection of books about black life.

This does not mean that we limit our reading to works by African Americans. I also recommend reading a variety of books, newspapers, and magazines. We need to keep current on world events and changes. All of these developments add to the base of education and knowledge we build. Education does not stop after the classroom; it continues

Education

throughout life. We must tap into this resource, and in turn, we will have more experiences and knowledge to use to improve black America.

In summary, we can take huge steps forward just by reading. Reading this book alone will help because it will add to your knowledge base. It will also qualify as the one book you, as an American, will read this year! Now imagine if you and your children continue to read more and more books. Am I saying that you should be like Ben Carson, and shoot for 104 books this year? Absolutely!

There is a cruel joke about black people (men in particular) that says if you want to hide something from us, you should put it in a book. The implied joke is that we do not like to read. So for the sake of argument, let's say that this fallacy is a true statement. What are we going to do about it? The more we read, the more educated we will be so that we can take advantage of greater opportunities. The choice is ours. To read or not to read: that is the question!

WAKE UP BLACK AMERICA! Read, read, and read even more!

WAKE UP! 42 Ways to Improve Black America NOW!

#10 Stress the Importance of Education

When the great Oprah Winfrey aired her show about the school she built in South Africa, I couldn't help myself, I had to cry. Her school gives young South African girls a safe learning environment and an opportunity to receive a good education. The girls selected to go to the school had many difficult obstacles to overcome. Some didn't have running water. Others lacked electricity; others had to walk long distances to get to basic necessities. Still others were threatened by thieves and sexual predators, while just trying to get to school. They knew that an education is the only way to rise above all of their problems. Despite their hardships, nothing could stand in the way of them getting to school.

The bottom line is: the girls at Oprah's school did not have the advantages that we take for granted. In the poorest African-American communities, we can find a clean water supply and electricity. The schools may not be the greatest, yet our children can get to them by bus or other form of transportation. Although some of our neighborhoods are ravaged with crime, our children can commute to school without constant fear of being attacked. In other words, we have advantages that we take for granted. This has created an apathetic atmosphere toward the educational process. It's far easier for our children to get an education than for many of the world's children.

In the black community, we have been battling apathy toward education and ridiculous stereotypes as well. For some odd reason, being educated has become synonymous with being "white." If you can speak English correctly, you are acting "white." If you know about a certain body of knowledge, say classical music or the arts, you are trying to be "white." A different way to look this is it portrays the feeling that we are such an inferior race that we are not capable of learning because we are black! It also devalues being educated. Some African Americans don't want to be considered educated or "white", while others will criticize if you are educated or "acting white."

Education

We have shattered these myths years ago, yet we still cling to the ideas. I suppose being educated is not in our makeup; we couldn't possibly come from the hood and be intelligent. This is pure nonsense and foolishness! The sad part about it is I have seen people of other races buy into this stereotype as well. A perfect example was when I was in graduate school and we had a contest about geography. In my class I was the ONLY African American out of about 25 students. The thought never crossed my mind that I would be acting "white" if I actually won.

We each received a blank map and had to label 20 countries around the world. After the scores were tallied, one student correctly identified 18 out of 20 countries. I think the professor purposely had the class try to figure out who this person was. People pointed out all of the so-called smartest people in the class. I was not one of them, yet I knew that there were only 3 that I had a problem identifying. No one thought about the remote possibility of me winning. The prize was a study atlas; compete with maps, facts, and figures.

Let's just say that a study atlas of the world sits on a shelf in my home. I still look at it just to learn more about the countries of the world. It was priceless when the professor called my name as the winner. The looks on my classmates' faces were priceless. Their jaws dropped, as if I had no right to be more "intelligent" than them. What, there is a black person who knows geography? Where's the value in that? I know that there is value in being educated. I also know that there are many African Americans who know more abut geography than me.

This is the reason why I believe in learning things just for the sake of being educated. We should learn everything we possibly can. Learning about topics that may not interest us makes the possibilities endless. The knowledge we acquire is all vital and important to our growth and unlimited potential. This is the value of education. It opens doors and lets us see beyond our present circumstances. Education creates equality; it gives a sense of belonging. Education builds self-respect and self-confidence. Education is a source of pride, and this can change the world!

WAKE UP! 42 Ways to Improve Black America NOW!

What made the children in South Africa battle against overwhelming odds everyday to get an education? Why do they see the value of an education? Why do they cling to their education as a way to improve their lot in life? Maybe it's because they want to be educated because it's the ONLY way to improve their lives. It's the only way to get what they want. They also had something that a lot of children in black American communities do not: the vision that education is the last hope for a better life.

WAKE UP BLACK AMERICA! Stress the importance of education!

Education

#11 Be Active in Your Children's Education

Looking back on the Oprah Winfrey special, most of the girls invited to study at her school had a parent, grandparent, or older sibling that pushed them. They encouraged their children to get an education. They could see the value in it. Although many of them had limitations on their ability to travel, many still showed up at the school when their children were accepted. They were willing to be a part of their children's education. It was not a choice; it was a necessity.

Now let's flip the script. Unfortunately, in many black American communities there is a lack of support for our children's education. Parents don't go to many of their children's school functions, often due to working a second job. Others just don't go at all. As a teacher, I had to go to report card nights to meet parents and discuss grades. Less than half of the parents ever came. Meanwhile, at home doing homework is not a priority.

Also, I was surprised by the amount of homework that was not done by students. I was shocked by parents who never asked their children about their schoolwork. They had no idea about the grades their children were earning! If you don't worry about your children's education, neither will they. As a parent, guardian, or other family member, you should include the following activities to insure that your child is getting a good education:

-attend parent-teacher conferences
-read school literature to find out what's happening
-help your child with homework/check homework daily
-check for tests and projects weekly
-attend your child's extracurricular activities
-assign additional reading at home
-find a good summer camp or program
-add value to education through real life examples

WAKE UP! 42 Ways to Improve Black America NOW!

The way to ensure that our schools are educating our children is through parental involvement. Parents should be aware of the school system and the work their child receives from the school. Parents can keep tabs on the school system by attending parent-teacher conferences to find out what happens in the classroom. They should get to know the teachers and administrators of the school. This makes it easier to resolve any issues that occur. Parents should also read any information that the school puts out.

Parents should also be involved in their child's academics. We should be helping our children with homework. Parents should check their children's assignments and tests daily. Parents should attend all school functions, from concerts to sports events involving the children. This support shows the child that the parent is aware, and checking on their activities. We should also encourage our children to participate in school activities. They can develop skills like teamwork and responsibility that will help them grow and develop.

Another way to be active in your child's education is by showing that education has value outside of the classroom. By assigning readings to children, it allows children to choose subjects that interest them for additional learning. Education should not end when summer break begins. Summer programs are a good way to keep your kids active, while sliding in a little studying as well. Most larger cities have free summer activities if paying for a more structured summer camp is not an option.

Another step is to add value to education through real world examples. A good way to do this is by using everyday experiences. Give kids activities to apply what they learn such as using a measuring cup to mix ingredients, reading a newspaper ad to compare prices, or one of those home science projects, like growing a small plant in a cup. Anything that our children can learn is worthwhile.

WAKE UP BLACK AMERICA! Be active in your children's education!

Education

#12 Think About Higher Education

As black Americans, we need to be aware of the importance of getting a higher education. As with speaking properly, it is unfortunate that going to college is sometimes considered acting "white". This too makes absolutely no sense. Going to college should be viewed for what it is: an opportunity to become successful. It is also an opportunity to expand knowledge, find a job, and support a family.

We must first understand why it is important to go to college. Statistics show that a college graduate earns on average four times more throughout their lifetime than a person who does not enter college. Of course, there are many variables that affect this reasoning, including the level of education completed by both. The numbers could change drastically if one person never earns a high school degree or the other earns an advanced college degree.

Another statistic that bears thought is the number of black males in prisons versus the number of black males in college. According to reports, the number of black males in prison exceeds the number of black males in colleges by 188,000 (Justice Policy Institute). All it takes is a short walk around the campus of any HBCU (Historically Black Colleges and Universities) to see many black males; then you can use your imagination to figure out how many more black men are incarcerated! This shows a crisis in our communities: so many black men have a smaller chance at being successful because they are not developing the skills that colleges teach.

We all know the repercussions of these statistics. Because many people of our race do not think about higher education for themselves and their children, our neighborhoods suffer. We have a shortage of educated black men and women who can solve the problems that plague our communities. So, each person's desire to get a college education has an effect on all of us. It also has an effect on our children; if they see an

WAKE UP! 42 Ways to Improve Black America NOW!

adult role model get a college degree, then they will be more likely to follow in the adult's footsteps.

Everyone has a role to play in this. We must stop downplaying the importance of education as trying to act "white". This stigma has quite an impact. Sometimes we allow others' thoughts and feelings to alter our actions, usually in a negative way. For example, for years I chose to be careful when discussing my college experiences and degrees. This was because most of the people I know never went to college. I really felt guilty about my own success, but this was really a selfish act on my part. I could have acted as a role model to encourage others to think about higher education.

We must help each other in this regard. Those who are in college, or have already graduated, need to spread the news about the benefits of higher education. It is surprising to see how many people write off a college education because they feel they can't make it as if it is not meant for them. However, nothing can be further from the truth. We must instill the right attitude about going to college and its benefits early on in our children's lives. Then we must keep our children focused on doing whatever it takes to get their college education.

We also need to be aware of the rising costs of obtaining a college education. It is expensive, but not impossible to go to college. We must save money for our children while they are young. This way, the rising costs of going to college will not be as daunting once our children are ready to go. We must also get our children to work hard academically to be prepared for the work they will receive in college. It can also lead to academic scholarships that can help pay some of the costs of going to college.

Influential African Americans have been helpful in promoting higher education. This must continue. It would be fantastic if more blacks stepped up and offered scholarships and mentoring opportunities for others. They could also do more public service announcements and commercials. When I was younger, some of the most influential

Education

commercials were for the United Negro College Fund. After all, a mind is still a terrible thing to waste. Once we get back to believing this, we can work towards our goals of being successful. Thinking about a college education is a good place to start.

WAKE UP BLACK AMERICA! Think about higher education!

WAKE UP! 42 Ways to Improve Black America NOW!

#13 Do Your Homework

Another way to be educated is to learn how to do research. It's a simple thing to do, yet we tend to be selective when trying to find out about things. For example, before you travel, you should find out what the places you want to visit have to offer. You should also do things like finding the correct route, places to stay, and the costs of taking the trip. This is all doing research. Most people would have no problem doing this.

However, how many people do their research in the following situations:

When applying for a credit card?
When accepting a job?
When selecting a school for our children?

In the first example, most people apply for, receive, and use credit cards without understanding the basics of how they work. Improper usage of a credit card can increase its interest rate. A credit card with a high interest rate can result in years of unnecessary interest payments. Unfortunately, years of interest payments have been hurting black folks' pockets for a long time.

In another example, most people accept jobs without doing thorough research. Doing research on a job means a lot more than checking out the environment when interviewing, or looking at a website for information. A step that few people take is talking to current employees who are not involved in the hiring process about their experiences on the job. This is a good way for African Americans to understand the dynamics of the work environment. Is the atmosphere good for blacks? Do we receive a fair shot at raises and promotions? Research can answer a lot of questions and prevent a poor choice when job seeking.

Finally, how many of us research schools before we send our children to them? Some inner city schools are suffering because of various issues

Education

like poor student performance and violence. Statistics are readily available about school districts and the performance of their schools. On the flip side, statistics are also available for the successful schools in our community. These things should be researched before a child is sent to a school. Also, if your school district has strict rules that state that we must send our children to the closest public school, then maybe that should be a consideration before we move into, or stay in, a given neighborhood.

We should not be content with researching things to find answers. We should also verify those answers to make sure they are accurate. Too many times, we are misled by faulty information from poor sources. Unfortunately, people are usually the reason why poor information spreads. In essence, African Americans should research the sources of own research whenever possible. Verify everything first, then make the best decision.

These are only a handful out of many situations when black people can benefit from educating ourselves by doing our research. We have so many opportunities that we should not settle for anything until we thoroughly check it out. In each situation, a poor decision can impact our lives for years. This will save us time, money, and wasted effort on things that do not advance our race. Yes, research may take extra time and effort, but it is well worth the trouble black America.

Remember that one of the most important topics that we must research to learn and thoroughly comprehend is our history as a race. Unfortunately, many African Americans do not know our history in the United States, let alone in Africa and the rest of the world. We need to research and discover these truths to learn our glorious past history. We must also research so that we can continue to make history. When we look at ourselves and we must learn how to use research to preserve and protect our future generations.

As a final thought, when is the best time for us to do our homework? The answer is easy: every day. Every day we should be doing things that

WAKE UP! 42 Ways to Improve Black America NOW!

requires research. This includes daily activities like checking homework, reading about current events, and grocery shopping. African Americans can learn a lot by carefully completing tasks like these.

WAKE UP BLACK AMERICA! Do your research everyday!

Education

#14 Learn About Your Health and Well Being

One of the most important things African Americans can do is learn more about our health. Looking at some of the key statistics relating to our health, such as obesity, HIV and AIDS cases, and cancer-related deaths, makes it clear that we need to do our homework. We need to be aware of each of the most dangerous health-related issues, and then prepare ourselves to avoid them. We need to build our knowledge so we can raise stronger families and communities. Not only that, but healthier African Americans are more productive African Americans.

Reading more about our health and well being is very important for African Americans. We can start with the foods we consume. When was the last time you read the ingredients of the food you ate? What are the ingredients of peanut butter and does it have nutritional value that can benefit our children? What is the proper temperature to cook ground beef? The answers can be found by reading the labels on the foods we eat. However, to gain a deeper understanding of what we consume, we need to learn about what things are good for the body and what things are not. Then our job is to increase our consumption of nutritious items and decrease the consumption of harmful ones.

As we all know, the things that taste the best usually aren't the best things for us to eat. It is true that many African Americans love to indulge in fried foods. We eat fried chicken, fried potatoes, French fries, and fried fish, just to name a few. I recently saw fried Oreo cookies, but hopefully no one you know has taken it this far! However, do we know and understand what these foods are doing to our bodies? All of this fried and greasy food contributes to higher cholesterol levels and heart-related illnesses.

Do not forget about the amounts of fast food we eat. Under a lot of pressure from various groups, fast food establishments and traditional restaurants have listed the calories and in some cases, ingredients of the meals they sell. This is to assure the public that their food is healthy.

WAKE UP! 42 Ways to Improve Black America NOW!

Even in those cases when their caloric standards are not good enough, they have gone to offering healthy alternatives or distinct menu choices. If we think about it, why would they need to offer these choices UNLESS the regular menu lacks some sort of nutritional value?

Speaking of fast food: can there be anything on the menu that is healthy at a restaurant that sells pizza, chicken, ribs, burgers, and ice cream? This is exactly what we see when looking at various establishments in African-American communities. There is also a rash of pseudo Chinese restaurants that serve "traditional" Chinese dishes, fried chicken wings, and French fries. Both of these places are usually open late at night, so they are a draw after other places close. Right off the bat, we can say that eating these items late at night can't possibly be healthy.

The next thing we need to learn about and understand is the diseases that impact the African-American community. Many suffer from high blood pressure. However, do we really know what it is and how to prevent it? High blood pressure, also known as the silent killer, is caused by a restriction of blood flowing through the body. This can be caused by having irregularities in the circulation system that need medical attention. However, more often than not it is caused by high cholesterol.

Cholesterol can stick to the walls of the arteries, making blood flow restricted. Over time, this can cause the heart to work harder to pump blood. As wonderful a machine as the heart is, it has the potential to "break down" under such conditions. We should read and learn more about high blood pressure and have it treated as soon as it is discovered. Also, if you have high levels of stress, chances are that your blood pressure will be higher.

High blood pressure can lead to a stroke, or a heart failure. Many icons of black America, like Luther Vandross, have suffered from a stroke or heart attack. In fact, it is a safe bet that most African Americans know someone who has experienced a stroke in their lifetime. We must learn how to eat properly and exercise regularly as ways to cut down our chances of being struck down. Although many stroke and heart attack

Education

victims do survive, their risk for having another episode increases.

When African Americans, especially those in the older generations, hear the word sugar, they think of a common disease. Sugar is another name for diabetes, and it affects us in great numbers. Diabetes is when the body does not produce normal levels of insulin, which helps the body perform many functions. There are many factors that cause diabetes such as genetics. Therefore, we should be aware of our genetic disposition to getting diabetes as soon as possible. A second common cause of diabetes is obesity. A common solution to this is increased physical activity.

Although illnesses such as high blood pressure and diabetes are terrible, in my opinion, they are not the most alarming health issues for African Americans. The amount of our brothers and sisters being infected with HIV and AIDS is an epidemic! These two sexually-transmitted diseases are tearing through our communities. The problem is that people still do not know enough about the diseases to prevent their spread. This must be addressed through education and awareness.

HIV refers to a virus that attacks the immune system's ability to ward off disease. AIDS is the result of the virus at its later stages. People can live with HIV for years before it becomes full blown AIDS. The issue is avoiding contracting HIV. What we don't know is how many African Americans are infected. It is because of this that slowly but surely, we are losing a part of a generation of African Americans to HIV and AIDS.

These are just the tip of the iceberg when it comes to African Americans and our health and well being. At the very least, we need to read and learn more about the unique health challenges we face in our lifetimes. Going to doctor's on regular visits and when there is a problem is another step. Finally, educating others is also a necessity. We can't be successful if we succumb to illnesses due to our lack of knowledge about our health.

WAKE UP BLACK AMERICA! Learn more about your health today and every day!

WAKE UP! 42 Ways to Improve Black America NOW!

SELF MOTIVATION: A KEY TO WAKING UP BLACK AMERICA!
❖ ❖ ❖

Now that we realize the importance of learning about our race and improving our education, we should have the understanding that we can become successful. At this point many people will hit a major roadblock: how do I get started? The answer is to become self motivated by learning the secrets that all successful people, regardless of race, background, or social status, have mastered. These secrets are easy to read, but difficult to learn and master.

If we want to be successful, raise our consciousness, become more productive, rebuild our communities, or accomplish any worthwhile goals, this chapter is the blueprint that we need to get started. We also need to teach our children these concepts early and often during their lives. This will allow them to have the confidence to take risks, the ability to handle adversity, and the strength to overcome challenges. Then, we can rebuild our neighborhoods, communities, and society. Self motivation is a key to building a better future for the African- American race.

15. Believe in a Higher Power
16. Join the Right Church
17. Keep the Faith
18. Use Four Mental Laws
19. Follow Your Senses
20. Positive Mental Outlook
21. Be Enthusiastic

Respect Our Story-Build Knowledge Through Education-Motivate Yourself

Self-Motivation

#15 Believe in a Higher Power

A few years ago I had a life changing experience while driving on the beloved Garden State Parkway in Jersey. If you have ever driven this road, you would know that some stretches are five lanes wide and always heavily congested. On this particular evening, I was in the middle lane doing about 70 mph when I spotted two cars in my rearview mirror approaching rapidly. They had to be doing 100 mph! The first car made a series of risky lane changes and the second followed suit. However, the second driver clipped a van. He careened across the roadway three times, hitting a guardrail twice and a concrete barrier. I witnessed this from about 100 yards behind so I had to slam on the brakes to avoid the debris from the quickly disintegrating vehicle.

At this point, several cars slowly crept through the darkness approaching the wreckage. Something told me to change lanes. I had no idea who, or what it was, but it told me to change lanes. The closer I got, the "louder" it was. Finally, I changed lanes, went on about another 50 feet, and then stopped almost where the mangled car came to rest. Other drivers were getting out of their cars, so I got out too. It was then that I realized why I had to change lanes: the driver of the car was lying in the road in the lane I was driving in, but I could not see him! We all stood in amazement because he was still breathing and somewhat responsive.

I have driven past that spot a few times since that night and I have seen a makeshift memorial there. My guess is that the driver died soon after the accident, but not because of me. The point of the story is: there is no doubt in my mind that I would have killed that man had I not listened to the voice that told me to change lanes. So who/what told me what to do? This is one of many reasons why I believe in a higher power.

It is the same for millions of African Americans worldwide who also believe in a higher power. We call Him God. Even though He has many names in many other faiths, the truth of the matter is He does exist. The proof is all around us and it can be traced throughout our experiences as

59

WAKE UP! 42 Ways to Improve Black America NOW!

a people. For example, if there is no God, then how did we survive the Middle Passage? How did we survive slavery? How did we survive Jim Crow, segregation, Civil Rights, and discrimination? These things alone should be enough proof for African Americans that there is a God.

Yet there are many of us who do not believe He exists. People who fall into this category are an interesting bunch. Just like so many people in Biblical times, they need to see signs that He is real. In fact, even after they see the signs, this may only provide a temporary belief in Him. However, what they do not realize is that the signs are always present, if we take the time and effort to look.

All we need to do is look at the wonders of nature to see God's power. I have seen ants walk in a straight line for 40 feet to get to a water supply, then march back in another line, as if on a two lane highway. Who gave them the ability to blaze this same trail with remarkable precision? Need more proof? If you drop a seed in the right ground and at the right time, it will produce. Who locked away the secret of production inside the seed? Need more proof? When the elements are right, a rain shower can produce a band of colors that stretch in a perfect arc. Who gave the rainbow all of the colors of the spectrum? The answer has to be God.

Meanwhile, there are even more African Americans who believe He exists, yet do not live up to His expectations of us, nor use the talents He has given us. In my opinion, this is worse than denying that He exists at all. He has given us the ability to dream, create, prosper, and serve. We all have these abilities, but far too many of us do not use them. Think about it: if you believe in an all-knowing, omnipresent, omnipotent God, then shouldn't this same God have the power to order our steps toward great things?

Many people lose sight of this, primarily due to everyday struggles and difficulties. It is during these times that even the most dedicated Christians can lose sight of God's plan. Some African Americans are an interesting case study in this regard. They go to church on Tuesday, Wednesday, and Sunday, read the Bible and pray daily, then lose faith

Self-Motivation

the minute something challenging comes along. Yet the God we serve does not want this; instead, He wants us to let Him work His divine plan through us, regardless of what we are facing.

This is an interesting part of this book, because it is not my place to make anyone a believer. It is entirely up to you! I believe that relationships with God, no matter how strong or weak, are an individual choice. A little guidance never hurts, but each African American should decide what relationship he or she will have with God. We must follow our own voices that tell us what to do when we can't, or refuse to, see what is in front of us. We must find calm, listen, and recognize when He is speaking.

Recently I found myself in a real predicament. I didn't have ANY money, and I had to get to and from work one more day before pay day. The problem was that my car was already on E and work was 24 miles away. Did I mention that the commute was 24 miles one way? However, I decided to go out on faith. I knew that getting there would not be a problem; getting back would be the hard part! Sure enough, I made it there. As I got back into the car to go home, the gas needle was well below E. I said a short prayer, waited in silence for about two minutes, then proceeded home without a problem. In fact, the needle did not move at all.

How did I know I would make it? It was because I believe in God! The truth is that there are millions of African Americans far more religious than me, but there are not too many who have more faith! My faith and belief tells me that even in my darkest hours (and there have been some blackouts) God will see me through. He will show me what I need to do to reach my unlimited potential, and then help others do the same. He has always had a plan for me; unfortunately, I didn't get with the program until recently. My question is: are you with the program yet?

WAKE UP BLACK AMERICA! Do you believe in God and His plan for you?

WAKE UP! 42 Ways to Improve Black America NOW!

#16 Find the Right Church Home

We all know how important the church is in African American communities. For millions of African Americans, the church is the pillar of our everyday lives. However, it is a shame that this very important part of the African-American experience is often ignored as if it doesn't exist. We know for a fact that Sunday mornings in our communities are reserved for church. So are Sunday afternoons, Tuesday evenings, Wednesday evenings, and occasionally Thursday evenings as well. One thing is for sure: black people attend church on the regular!

This is why it is important for us to choose a church home where we can get what we need spiritually. In my opinion, church should be a sanctuary where we can escape everyday troubles and hardships and build our spiritual muscles. We need stronger spirits if we want to effectively deal with many of the issues in this book, from improved health to greater motivation. However, one of the saddest truths is that many African Americans go to churches weekly, yet do not receive the strength and guidance to improve their lives.

The bottom line is that choosing the right church should be high on your list of priorities. The question is how do you know when you have found your church home? Well we can start by discussing what it feels like when you are in the wrong place. I have visited many churches in my lifetime and have enough experience to know when there is a lack of spirit in the building. Often African American churches, especially older ones steeped in tradition, will be fulfilling to those who are longstanding members, yet offer little to someone looking for a church home.

Another sure sign of being in the wrong place is by looking at the leader of the church. How does the pastor carry himself or herself? How is the message they deliver? Does he or she give the appearance of being larger

Self-Motivation

than the church, or is he or she more of a messenger who follows the Word? As in any leadership position, pastors must hold themselves to a very high standard so that others can follow their lead. Far too often, especially in African- American churches, the pastor is not an effective leader. When this occurs, the experience of church is diminished.

Finally, you can tell if you are in the wrong church if the congregation is not being filled with the spirit. How can you tell this? All it takes is looking at the response of churchgoers to the Word, their love and sense of brotherhood for each other, and their attendance! Many churchgoers simply go through the motions. Others are not active attendees; instead, they are part- timers who participate when it is convenient.

If we can tell what being in the wrong church feels like, then surely we can describe what it feels like to be in the right house of worship. We can simply say the opposite of the previous list. Is the church stuck in neutral due to older traditions, or is it progressive? Is the pastor a truly called to lead, or is he into self promotion? Does the congregation thrive, or are they stuck in a spiritual rut? Yes we can answer these questions with a few visits to a given church.

I do believe that it is extremely hard to figure out when you have chosen the right church home. My answer to this dilemma is that you will know when you are in the right place. You will know when your spirit is being served and filled. You will know when you are growing and building faith. You will know when the spirit is present before, during, and after your church experiences. You will know when you are in the right place when you find whatever it is you are looking for in a church and the message being delivered.

For many African Americans, there is no greater joy than finding the right church home. The communality and brotherhood of a good church is impossible to find out in "the world." In fact, the relationships I personally have forged in church are the most treasured and fulfilling relationships I have. This is because I found the right church home. Even though I no longer live near my church home, I still consider it the right place for me.

The thought of African Americans who are in churches across the country where their spirits are not being fed is a problem. It is a problem because of the missed opportunities for growth for those people, and the church communities they are a part of. Another by product is the eventual lack of outreach and support outside the doors of the sanctuary. What a missed opportunity this is for our people!

The good news is that there are many churches across the country that are involved in the growth and spiritual maturity of their members and their communities. It is in these places where we need to congregate, plan, and promote spiritual growth and prosperity. As a result, we can have a major impact on society while bringing in those who need their spirits renewed. Yes, the African American church CAN and does have a leading role in raising the fortunes of our people far and wide.

As a final thought, I believe in God! Yet there are many African Americans who believe in other spiritual leaders and faiths. This is why I leave most religious discussions open for debate and interpretations. There is enough room, and certainly enough faith, for everyone, regardless of their spiritual belief system. My advice to African Americans is to simply believe in something greater than ourselves, who has a master plan for all of our lives. You can find out more about this master plan, if, and when, you find the right church home.

WAKE UP BLACK AMERICA! Find the right house of worship!

Self-Motivation

#17 Keep the Faith

Faith! The first thing that African Americans need to understand about faith is its true meaning. In the Bible in the Book of Hebrews, faith is defined as: the substance of things hoped for, the evidence of things not seen. What this means is simple: you have to have faith to believe that things can, and will happen, even when it looks as if they are impossible. This is when many people lose what it means to be faithful. They can't see the results they want, so they believe that they are not attainable.

Nothing is farther from the truth. Being faithful means to know and anticipate things that will come your way. Faith will bring you the things you want. However, there is a price to pay that goes hand in hand with faith: work! The Bible in the Book of James also says: faith without works is dead. Usually those who think they have faith fall short when the work comes into the equation. Unfortunately for some, faith and work are two ideas that do not go together.

What exactly does this mean for African Americans? It means that we, as individuals and as a group, can pull ourselves out of the dilemmas we presently face. First of all, it takes faith: an unwavering belief that we can live up to our unlimited potential. Second, it takes work: a burning desire to do whatever it takes to achieve what we want. This powerful combination is a force, ordained by God, that can't be prevented or stopped. When we start to understand this, we will be able to improve our lot in society.

Do you believe that your wildest dreams can come true? Most people would say yes, yet their words and actions would tell a different story. It all goes back to childhood, when children are allowed to dream. We ask the age old question: what do you want to be when you grow up? No matter how wild the answers to these questions are, to the child, they are attainable. They have a belief system already in place from birth. It is called faith.

WAKE UP! 42 Ways to Improve Black America NOW!

As this child grows up, they experience the ups and downs of maturity. They develop a sense of what is "possible" versus what is "impossible". They see their parents, other adults, and their own peers in situations that can cloud their belief system. They look at their circumstances, community, society, and world to reinforce their growing negative perception of reality. As this happens, their faith begins to waver. They begin to walk by sight.

Faith does not walk by sight, it walks by possibilities. Faith has NOTHING to do with your present situation, what your friends and family tells you or the amount of money in your pocket. Faith does not care about any of these things. Instead, it focuses on the future that you can not see. It focuses on opportunities. It focuses on our God- given ability to produce results beyond your wildest dreams as a child.

If we think about it, EVERYTHING starts with a dream. The dream becomes a vision. The vision becomes an idea. The idea becomes a plan. The plan becomes and action. The action becomes a result. Faith propels this process every step of the way. It must be present as we move from one phase to the next. If we lose faith in the dream, it will never become a vision. If we lose faith in the plan, it will never become an action.

The obvious question that African Americans must ask is: how do we keep the faith? There are many different answers; however, some are more important than others. The first answer to the question is to seek God and His guidance. Regardless of how you get into His presence, we should all understand that this should be our daily goal. God has established in all of us the ability to make our dreams come true. In return, He asks us to have faith. He asks us to believe. He asks us for the dream, vision, idea, plan, and most importantly, the ACTION. He asks us to WORK!

Secondly, African Americans can keep the faith by believing that we can achieve our goals. We can't afford to lose sight of what we want to accomplish. It doesn't matter what it looks like today; it can be a totally different picture tomorrow. Once again, it requires work. If we can

Self-Motivation

refocus on our goals when the hour is darkest, then we can work toward changing our reality. Faith needs to be strongest when we are at our lowest points.

We can keep the faith by a simple, yet forgotten idea: keeping things to ourselves. How many times have you come up with a dream, vision, and idea, told someone, and received a less than supportive reaction? This can strangle your faith and prevent you from making a plan and taking action. Many of lose sight because we tell others about our plans. Sometimes you have to keep it to yourself until you are well into the action/work phase of the process.

Another way to keep the faith is to learn about how other African Americans defied the odds to achieve greatness. They did not give up; they kept the faith. Let's think about it, what would have happened if Rosa Parks would have given up on that bus in Montgomery? What would have happened if Booker T. Washington would have given up as he slept on city streets? What would have happened if George Washington Carver would have given up after his first unsuccessful attempt at finding different uses for the peanut?

Hopefully, the lesson about faith will become a part of our daily lives. Sometimes we feel as if we have nothing. However, we have so much more. We have God, so we need to remember that HE has a plan for us. We have potential, so we need to build the strength to work toward it. We have faith, so we need to summon the courage to look for it. Faith moves mountains. Faith builds bridges. Faith is the substance of things hoped for, but not yet seen.

WAKE UP BLACK AMERICA! Remember to keep the faith!

#18 Use Four Mental Laws

The laws we are all aware of are the laws created by man. However, there is another set of laws that exist that we should be aware of: mental laws. Proper application of these four concepts will change the fortunes of black America. Some African Americans will not agree with the concepts explained here. This is because they will not explore the concepts with an open mind. Instead, they will use their preconceived notions and current situations to cloud their judgment.

This is not the right approach. The mental laws exist and they are timeless. They are also keys to becoming successful and achieving goals for millions of people. In fact, as we study the highest achievers of our race, we learn that they believe in these four mental laws and put them into practice. The four mental laws are a major part of their success. Once again, if we all learn and apply these concepts, they will lead to success.

The best ways to learn the laws that follow is the old fashioned way: read the definition followed by an example. The reader should put some thought into each law and understand the power and impact of each concept. Then, the laws should be tested, either by putting in your own examples or looking out for the laws at work in the future.

Law of Attraction

The law of attraction means we have the ability to bring into existence the things we want in life. The law of attraction works like magnets. Two magnets will align and attach to each other on given sides based on their magnetism. The law works in various ways in life but the concept remains the same: each and every person can get whatever they want in life. This should be read again. We all are "magnets" who have the ability to attract the things we want.

Self-Motivation

An example of the law of attraction is my beautiful wife Belinda. When I was very young, I used to say that I wanted a wife who fit the following description: intelligent, caring, taller than average, lighter brown skin, and other features not to be mentioned here! In other words, I formed a PICTURE of who I wanted to marry. This is when the law kicks in. Just like a magnet, I attracted the person I wanted because Belinda fits my description perfectly.

I conditioned my mind to look for someone who fit the picture. In fact, whenever I found someone who did not fit the picture, it never worked out. It was like trying to fit a square peg in a round hole. It wasn't until I met the "girl of my dreams" that the law of attraction was fulfilled. Remember, the law must work in conjunction with itself: my wife had to have her own PICTURE of me and I fit her description too!

Many African Americans use the law of attraction to bring destructive things to existence. A poor education will attract poverty. Sexual irresponsibility will attract diseases or maybe even illegitimate children. Desire for materialistic things will attract spending too much or reliance on credit cards. Selling drugs will attract dangerous situations and incarceration. The answer to these and many other dilemmas our communities face is to learn how to attract positive things.

LEARN TO ATTRACT POSITIVE THINGS TO SEE POSITIVE RESULTS!

Law of Practice

The law of practice means that true success requires constant practice. Practice means work. We must put in our fair share of work to become successful. This is a timeless principle that is etched in stone. Everyone, regardless of race, who has achieved any goal, has used this concept. The law of practice can be best described by using an old saying: "practice makes perfect."

An example of the law of practice is my career as a motivational speaker.

WAKE UP! 42 Ways to Improve Black America NOW!

If asked 20 years ago about the probability of seeing myself speaking in front of large crowds, I would have said it was impossible. Public speaking was not my strong suit. However, time after time I had to speak in front of others throughout my education. Practicing by putting speeches together before presenting them made my speaking skills increase dramatically. Now it is easy to put together and present ideas in front of large audiences.

We as African Americans must understand that practice makes perfect. If we want to improve our lot in any aspect, it takes work. We can not expect our children to do well in school if they are not practicing it at home. We can not expect to improve our language if we are not practicing how to speak properly. We can not expect to expand our economic base if we are not practicing proper spending habits.

How do Venus and Serena Williams serve tennis balls over 120 miles per hour?

How did Tiger Woods become the best golfer in the world?

How does Denzel Washington produce mesmerizing performances in countless films?

How does Yolanda Adams sing songs to stir the soul and move the spirit?

PRACTICE AND YOU WILL SEE POSITIVE RESULTS IMMEDIATELY!

Law of Reciprocity

The law of reciprocity means what you give will come back to you abundantly. Giving is a concept that some African Americans do not understand. It is a powerful concept that we must tap into to become successful. Simply put, you get what you give. Another way to look at this law is karma: what comes around goes around. We must remember

Self-Motivation

two important points:

-you should NOT give ONLY because you will get something in return; instead give for the sake of helping others.

-you should not take from others and expect to get something in return; this never works.

An example of the law of reciprocity was when a lapse in judgment cost me dearly. It was about a month before Christmas and a woman dropped an envelope on the floor at my store. I picked it up and found money inside; about $500. Should I keep it or give it back? The woman looked like she had money. She was dressed in fine clothes and an expensive coat. Surely she didn't need the money as much as I did! After asking a coworker, I decided to keep the money.

That Christmas was great! I spent the extra money on gifts for everyone, including myself. I never thought about the lady who lost the money. What if it was all she had? What if she could not buy gifts for her loved ones? The law of reciprocity was about to strike me down. The next two years, unexpected expenses hit me hard, each occurring about a month before Christmas. As a result, my money was short and I could not afford to buy gifts. I managed to get a few things, but both holidays left me with an empty feeling. I did not give to get; in fact I didn't give anything, I took.

Keeping this principle in mind, the reason why our communities are suffering in many areas is a direct result of a lack of giving. We do not give enough to our schools, so they do not always turn out highly educated students. We do not give enough education and proper mentoring to our children, so they do not always become productive citizens. We do not give enough to charity, so people who need help do not always get what they need.

The African- American community can easily fix this by investing time, knowledge, and money back into our lives. If successful black people in

WAKE UP! 42 Ways to Improve Black America NOW!

each community could donate a little more time to mentor children, their behaviors and achievement would soar. If successful black people could donate a little more knowledge to others, our body of knowledge would expand. If successful black people could donate a little more money to the RIGHT causes, our communities could get the help they need.

GIVE ABUNDANTLY TO BE REWARDED FOR PROVIDING SERVICE!

Law of Expectancy

The law of expectancy means whatever you expect will come to pass in your life. It is perhaps the most powerful of the four laws. African Americans need to understand how this concept works for our benefit or our detriment. If you have high expectations, you will seek ways to fulfill those expectations. On the other hand, if you have low expectations, you will also seek ways to fulfill those expectations.

An example of the law of expectancy is one African American child I met while substitute teaching. He got into lots of trouble and rarely completed his work. It looked like his every move was scrutinized and he was lost. I had a chance to ask him a simple question: what's wrong? When he realized he could talk openly he gave me a shocking answer: no one thinks I can do anything! Here is a second grader affected by the law of expectancy. He felt his classmates and teacher thought he was dumb so he lived down to their expectations.

Later on that day, the class had an assignment. I made it my business to help this boy to finish it. It was difficult because he wanted to give up often. I told him to keep trying because I knew he could finish the work. Slowly, he wrote answers until he finished. I told him to go and show his teacher. When he did, I learned something else. Based on her reaction, there was validity to his opinion because the teacher was surprised that he was able to finish!

African Americans can learn a valuable lesson from this. We must expect

Self-Motivation

more from our children so they can be successful. A good way to raise expectations is to tell our children they can do better, then reward them when the do. They will be more likely to try harder and do better in school. The law of expectancy works; if you expect success, you will achieve success.

Low expectations have our children standing on corners being unproductive. Low expectations have people finding reasons why it can't be done. Low expectations have people turning to drugs and alcohol as a way out. Low expectations have people blaming their social, political, and economic situations on the fact that they are black.

EXPECT SUCCESS AND YOU WILL BECOME SUCCESSFUL!

There are many other mental laws that have been proven to be keys to success. We should study each of them to unlock power that our race needs today. In my opinion, books written by Dennis Kimbro, an African-American author, are the best resource for learning more about the mental laws. His books, along with works by Napoleon Hill should be staples in every African American's home library.

WAKE UP BLACK AMERICA! Understand how to follow the mental laws!

WAKE UP! 42 Ways to Improve Black America NOW!

#19 Be Aware of Your Five Senses

Throughout our lives, we have been taught to trust our senses. Upon a quick review, we can see how this can be bad advice. Your eyes can look upward and see a sun that appears to fit in the palm of your hand, when in reality it is so much bigger. You nose can smell a given scent, but incorrectly identify what it is. Close your eyes and touch an object: sometimes you can guess what it is, sometimes you can't. So while we can question these natural senses, there are other senses that we should not question once we identify what they mean.

Sense of Purpose

How many African Americans know what their sense of purpose is? Why are you here? If you can answer either of these questions, then you probably have a pretty good idea what your sense of purpose is. I believe that we should spend our first 20 years or so identifying what we want to do with our lives. This is based on our upbringing, friendships, and educational background. Usually, once we get through the college experience, then we should start to focus on goals. We should spend the next 5-10 years in training for fulfilling our sense of purpose. By 30, our plans for the realization on our mission should be in full bloom.

African Americans who get in their 30s and beyond, but still do not know their purpose, should regroup, refocus, and redirect their energy. At this point, the question to ask is: what is my passion? For some, it may take missing the mark, and spending many years after college in the wilderness. This is common, but not acceptable. It requires an honest, self- examination of ways to get back on track to head toward our sense of purpose. It is never too late to start over, especially when you can identify your passion and sense of purpose. As a final thought, African Americans should not be afraid of change.

Self-Motivation

Sense of Direction

Speaking of change, it is required when we no longer know our sense of direction. In fact, quite a few African Americans do not have a sense of direction. A sense of direction requires a road map so that we know how to get to our destination. In other words, now that we have a sense of purpose, how do we get to it? This is where planning and organization come into play. We need to learn how to plan, change course, and remain detail- oriented to keep moving in the right direction.

Our lives can be compared to a ship sailing on the ocean. The ship has a destination in mind. It has a well planned and plotted course, yet it can change that course should storms appear on the horizon. If the ship follows this plan, it will reach its destination safely. In the case of African Americans, how many of us have plotted our course? If we can't plot an accurate course, then how can we know where we are on the journey or if we will make it to our destination? We need a sense of direction to achieve our goals.

Sense of Pride and Self Worth

The recipe for success for African Americans includes a sense of pride in everything that we do. If pride is missing, then chances are we are not performing at our best. It means we are not living up to our God-given potential. For example, we should have a sense of pride in our work. It really doesn't matter if you build monuments or sweep the streets around them. The builder should strive to have to most remarkable structures ever created. At the same time, the street sweeper should strive to have the cleanest sidewalks ever stepped on. We should take pride in the tasks that we perform: all the time, every time.

Another sense we should posses is a sense of self worth. Every life has a purpose; every life has value. Our Creator has given each and every African American the ability to use their talents to the fullest. The problem occurs when we do not see, or believe, in our self worth. The architect and the street sweeper have equal worth. Both of them can

WAKE UP! 42 Ways to Improve Black America NOW!

serve their purpose and produce outstanding results. However, does the sweeper believe in his worth as much as the architect? Our society assigns value to people according to their status and material possessions, yet we can't fall into this trap. Each African American has tremendous value and worth to our community.

Common Sense

How many times have we seen others make decisions that simply don't make sense? It seems like an everyday occurrence when we can point the finger at someone who seems like they lack common sense. If you can't find these people, then it is probably you! However, this applies in some way to all of us, so we are equally responsible for not using our common sense. For example, common sense would tell you to call the bill collector, or accept their call, to set up some type of payment arrangements. How many of us, myself included, have avoided collection calls? Meanwhile the problem keeps getting bigger and bigger until it becomes so severe that it must be faced and dealt with.

African Americans deal with common sense issues far more complicated than avoiding creditors. We know that there are a lot of black children born out of wedlock, yet we keep having unprotected sex. We know that we are more likely to have high blood pressure, yet we can't get enough of fried foods. We know we are more likely to drop out of school, yet we don't emphasize the importance of getting an education. These are common sense issues, yet we as a people struggle with them. If we want to improve our lives, we must use more common sense.

Dollars and Sense

For African Americans, dollars and sense don't always go together. We know how many of our brothers love to have fancy cars, and then park them in front of the projects. Many of our ladies love the carry a $250 purse, and then put $10 inside it. Neither of these examples shows how to use dollars with sense. We could drive a more reasonable car, while working on improving where we live. We could carry a less expensive

Self-Motivation

purse, while increasing the amount of money for saving. Money moves like these show financial irresponsibility.

When will we learn to use sense when spending our dollars? We can start by tithing, which means giving the first tenth of our money back to God. We can save and invest our money. We can recycle our dollars by patronizing institutions in our neighborhoods run by our people. We can also live within our means and avoid overusing credit cards. Finally, we can plan for our children's college education and our own retirement. These things illustrate some of a number of ways we can better manage our money. When we practice these habits on a regular basis, then we can say that we are using our dollars wisely and making a lot of sense.

WAKE UP BLACK AMERICA! Trust your five senses!

WAKE UP! 42 Ways to Improve Black America NOW!

#20 Develop a Positive Mental Outlook

Walking down the street in my community painted a dark picture of African-American people. They tended to have hard looks; their faces filled with anger and despair. Chances are, if they fit this description, they were unhappy with their current state of affairs. However, there is a method that can change their outlook on life. It changes the way people look at situations and events that take place in their lives. It is having a positive mental outlook.

People who have a positive mental outlook are few and far between because most people are negative. Most people look for bad things to happen, make them happen, then claim that their theory of impending doom was correct. What many people do not realize is the process works in reverse as well. If you look for good things to happen and make them happen, then you can claim that things will work out well. It is all based on your mental outlook.

Have you ever noticed how some people can find good in everything? They look for and find a silver lining in every situation. Even on rainy days they can find something positive to think about. Their secret is simple: they have a positive mental outlook! The best part is that we all have the ability to have a positive outlook too. Black Americans need to harness this power in order to improve our daily affairs.

Try the following experiment:

Think about the worst thing that has happened to you this week. Now try to find something positive that can happen, or already has happened as a result of that bad experience. The truth is that if you dig deep enough, there HAS TO BE something positive you can take out of your worst experience.

How many people who tried this experiment could not find or struggled to find a positive result?

Self-Motivation

Moving on, I certainly hope that race is not a factor in having a positive outlook. However, it must be said that many black people tend to be less positive because of our past history and hardships. They do not see reasons to be hopeful. You can tell just by looking in people's faces. They think that the world is against them. They do not understand that there is a way to change the outlook of any situation: A SMILE!

If we learn to smile, we can make any situation better. A smile lightens the load regardless of the issue. It helps to relax the body and it gives off positive vibes. There is an old concept that pertains to smiling: if you give someone an honest smile, they will respond with a smile. In fact, smiling is contagious; it catches on quick. Besides, if someone has a hard time smiling, they are probably not a person you want to have around anyway. They probably have a negative attitude.

African Americans need to understand the power of being positive. A positive outlook is a huge step to becoming successful. We have to learn to believe that we can be successful in life; therefore, negative thoughts should be avoided at all costs. In fact, take negative things out of your life completely. The most important thing to take away is the word failure. Avoid using the word! Avoid saying the word! Avoid writing the word! Avoiding failure is a positive step toward a positive outlook.

Another thing to consider is the attitudes of others. Others who have some influence in your life can easily turn your new found positive outlook into a negative outlook. These people should be avoided as much as possible. Their outlook is negative, so if they can change your attitude to negative also, then the law of attraction will kick in. As we will address in an upcoming chapter, this is why we must learn to surround ourselves with positive people.

Black Americans must look for the positive people in our communities if we want to develop a positive outlook. We must look for the positive institutions in our communities if we want to develop a positive outlook. We must read positive literature if we want to develop a positive outlook. We must watch and support positive television, film, and music if we

WAKE UP! 42 Ways to Improve Black America NOW!

want to develop a positive outlook. All of these things are keys to having a positive presence in our communities that will spread to other African Americans.

WAKE UP BLACK AMERICA! Develop a positive outlook today!

Self-Motivation

#21 Be Enthusiastic

At a high school, a student was selected to read the morning announcements over the intercom system every day of the week. Usually, the readers were monotone and lifeless. One week an exciting, friendly voice boomed throughout the school with enthusiasm that bounced off the walls. It was a welcomed change of pace since most of us were still asleep at 8:15 am. However, most of the students hated her style of reading the announcements. Students offered many reasons why they disliked her announcements: "too happy", "too loud", or "fake because the information was boring and tired." They missed the point!

This is what is called a "teachable moment" in academic circles: a chance to address an issue on the spot, gather information, and offer solutions or alternative viewpoints. Since I enjoyed these moments, I tackled the issue of the student with other students. This particular student could take any information and make it interesting, fresh, and filled with ENTHUSIASM. It was different because she was a passionate person. Few of the students could relate to her because of their negative attitudes. The next day at 8:15 and for the rest of the week, the students groaned out loud as our enthusiastic student started the announcements...

It was my pleasure to teach this student for two years. Looking back, she was one of the most memorable students I have ever had. It was not because of her intelligence, looks, academic performance, or helpfulness. It was because of her eager attitude. She smiled a lot; and even though she experienced the ups and downs of being a teenager, she always came through rough times with a positive attitude. Understand, I'm sure she wasn't always positive, but in public, she always put on her best face regardless of the situation.

This precious young lady was well liked to her face, yet talked about often behind her back. I could tell that most of her "friendships" were not real because others found faults with her. The reason why was simple: they did not like her enthusiasm! Why are people like this? Why do some

WAKE UP! 42 Ways to Improve Black America NOW!

people dislike happy folks? This is another plague that runs rampant in the African American community, where people who are positive and happy are not acting black enough. They are not down with the struggle.

This is a silly way to look at having enthusiasm. Instead, we should actively seek out people, regardless of race, who have energy, passion, and drive. As stated earlier, this will prove to be a difficult task because most people think negatively. Enthusiasm rubs off on others, unless they are so negative that it blinds them. The law of attraction really works here. Enthusiastic African- American people will attract each other!

Most people can use enthusiasm in two distinct ways. There are some people who can find a silver lining in any situation. They are able to be enthusiastic because of and in spite of. They are positive people by nature, and they tend to stick to their positive beliefs regardless of what others think. They have strong convictions, and they get things they want because they are able to enthusiastically accept their results. They can even find unexpected benefits in the results they receive.

Others use enthusiasm when they find their passion. This is why everyone should identify their purpose in life. They understand what they are good at, and then they put all of their energy into it. Their enthusiasm is contagious; in fact, it is combustible! Their enthusiasm cannot be controlled. People who fit into this category are the highest achievers in our race. They are excited about their lives and look forward to their future.

African Americans appear to be the least enthusiastic people on earth! Just look at our people's faces. Check out our body language. Listen to the words we use. Take notice of how we describe the future. This even holds true in our daily activities. Some black folks are mad in the morning, upset by noon, angry after work, and frustrated at night. It's easy to see why we are not enthusiastic about our prospects for tomorrow. This is a trend that we must reverse if we are to continue to grow and prosper as a race.

Self-Motivation

How African Americans become more enthusiastic? If the question has crossed your mind and you do not have an answer, go back to page one and start again! We can start by learning our history and improving our education. We can move on to becoming self-motivated and improving our own lives. We can master the art of communication and support each other. Need a preview of what's to come? We can strengthen our families and our finances. We can offer and provide top notch service to our communities and society.

If you want to leave a lasting impression, stamp yourself in someone's memory by being enthusiastic. People who accentuate the positive stand out from the crowd. People who have passion stand out from the crowd. In both cases, enthusiasm carries them forward, and takes them to places most people will never go. What is the difference between these people and others? ENTHUSIASM!

WAKE UP BLACK AMERICA! Learn how to be enthusiastic!

WAKE UP! 42 Ways to Improve Black America NOW!

SELF-IMPROVEMENT: A KEY TO WAKING UP BLACK AMERICA!
❖ ❖ ❖ ❖

So far in our journey, we have learned more about our race, made a commitment to education, and become more self-motivated. The next step is to learn how each and every African American can improve their lives in order to live out their dreams. This process of self improvement is ongoing; it may require a lifetime of hard work and effort on our part. Yet it is so important because each and every African American who improves their life has a positive effect on all of us.

A common thread throughout this work is the concept of teaching these concepts to our children. We need to educate our children on the benefits of improving each and every day. However, this is one of those ideas that are impossible to teach unless you follow these behaviors yourself. The old "do as I say, not as I do" attitude will not work here. We must model these behaviors consistently in order to become successful. Let the games begin!

22. You Might as Well Excel
23. Develop and Use the IT Factor
24. Starve Yourself to Get Hungry
25. Write Down Your Goals/Set Time Limits
26. Control Your Destiny/Stay the Course
27. Accept Your Results/Do Something About Them
28. Keep Your Word/Honor Your Commitments

Respect Our Story- Build Knowledge Through Education- Motivate Yourself- Look for Ways to Improve Yourself

Self-Improvement

#22 You Might as Well Excel (Strive For Excellence)

Have you ever wondered why some people seem to get all of the breaks in life? The fact is that some people make things happen, while other wait for them to happen. These people are known as DOERS. Usually, a common trait that doers have is that they are the best at what they do or they are well on their way to becoming the best. How do they do it? They accomplish what they want because they want to be the best, regardless of their situation. People like this choose to excel; they strive for excellence.

In a former life, my job was driving a limousine. In this role, my goal was to strive for excellence by being the best limo driver in the company. After a year of learning and providing strong customer service, I became recognized as one of the top drivers. Whenever VIP clients needed a ride, only the top drivers were selected to cater to their needs. On a given night, Roger Clemens the future Baseball Hall of Famer needed a ride to and from a function. This function took place on the night before he made history: winning his 300th career game. The pressure to win his next game was mounting because of the significance of the achievement. He needed to relax and enjoy this occasion, then prepare for the next day's game. Guess who was selected to accompany Mr. Clemens?

Critics of this will say that the game of rewards and recognition is merely a popularity contest. Others will say they are passed over because of "politics'. Still others will say that those who play the game and brown nose make it to the top. While all of these things might be true, their effect is not as large as it seems. More often than not, those who win rewards and recognition are the ones who strive to excel. On the other hand, it is the critics who do not put forth enough extra effort so it seems like everyone is passing them by. I was selected to meet Roger Clemens, drive him around, and discuss his next game because I earned it!
My African American family, you might as well excel! When you strive

WAKE UP! 42 Ways to Improve Black America NOW!

to be the best, opportunities will find you. This is because work and action are both contagious and magnetic. You can attract things that seem out of reach by striving to be excellent. The process starts when someone does a task well. The RIGHT people will recognize this and appreciate the effort that they see. Then the RIGHT people, those who put forth similar effort, will join the cause or try to emulate what they see. Soon there is a shared movement toward excellence and achievement.

In the workplace, the concept of striving to excel is always in full display. Some African Americans understand the concept of pursuing excellence in the workplace. They understand that someone is paying them to do a GREAT job, not just a good one. Since that job is theirs, they have the belief that they might as well excel. While there, they take ownership of their job and its responsibilities. Excellence in the workplace demands taking ownership. It demands personal responsibility for positive results. It demands being a DOER!

Think about it for a second. When you have your own company, what kind of employees would you want? Would you want to pay employees who own their job and its responsibilities, or waste money on those who do not? Would you invest in people who complete tasks to the best of their ability, or would you rather have people who do not care for the quality of their work? Would you want employees who value time and use it wisely, or waste time?

Wasting time equals wasting opportunities. Wasting time equals wasting a chance to learn something new. Wasting time equals wasting a chance to improve a process. Wasting time equals wasting potential. Most importantly, wasting time equals wasting money. Those who waste time do not strive for excellence. My philosophy is that if you are not striving for excellence in your workplace, find somewhere else to work where you will!

All African Americans should desire being excellent for one particular reason. We all know that we have to work twice as long and twice as

Self-Improvement

hard just to prove that we belong. However, we can put these notions to rest by striving to be excellent, from the first impression we give, to the last greeting we offer on the way out. People will not question our intelligence, motives, or ability once we prove that we are striving for excellence all the time. This is another reason why we might as well excel.

The concept of striving for excellence is not exclusively for the workplace. The truth of the matter is that striving for excellence should become a daily habit that translates into many activities. African Americans should be excellent when communicating with each other. We use words correctly and expect the same in return. African Americans should be excellent when providing service to each other. We give outstanding customer service and receive it as well. African Americans should be excellent when handling our finances. We practice being financially responsible and saving more for the future.

Those who strive for excellence keep in mind the reason for being excellent: self-improvement. Attempting to be the best at something should not occur at the expense of others. We should not get involved in attacking others, endless comparisons, jealousy, envy, or spiteful behavior. These behaviors waste time and effort; therefore, they cannot be a part of the process of striving for excellence. Those who strive for excellence put in their best effort. We can figure out whether or not we are being our best by looking at a few traits.

As a reminder, African Americans who strive for excellence…

Do not waste time

Do not gossip or assassinate people's character

Do not dismiss new ideas without trying them first

Do not compare their rewards, or lack of recognition, to others

WAKE UP! 42 Ways to Improve Black America NOW!

Do not complete tasks only to be rewarded or recognized

Do not change their ethics or lower their standards to be the best

WAKE UP BLACK AMERICA! You might as well excel!

Self-Improvement

#23 Develop and Use Your IT Factor

There are many African Americans who have a unique blend of intelligence, compassion, and positive energy. They are driven, focused, and committed to excellence. They are winners and they encourage others to be winners too. What do these people have? I call this the IT factor. Those who have the IT factor have attitudes that are contagious to some people, curious to others, and intolerable to most. Their attitudes are intolerable because so many people are negative. Despite this, people who have the IT factor are very attractive and find their way to success. So what is it that makes people who have the IT factor so attractive?

The answer to this question is that everyone wants to have the IT factor. All of the traits these people possess are universally accepted and admired. They are the traits that we all want to have and use to our advantage. Yet reality is that some African Americans do not have many of these qualities. However, the good news is that most people possess some of the qualities that those with the IT factor possess. There is even better news. The qualities we do not possess can be learned and put into practice.

African Americans with the IT factor can amaze us with their intelligence. It is a wonderful thing to witness an intelligent black woman or man in action. What we all need to understand is that their knowledge was gained overnight. They were probably inclined to excel academically at an early age. This trend continued through their formal education and perhaps their college experiences too. In other words, their intelligence is based on a commitment, made at an early age, to take education seriously. This is a trait that all of us can put into practice immediately.

African Americans who have the IT factor are some of the most caring and compassionate people we will ever meet. They are in tune to helping and serving others. They are good listeners who know how to give support and advice. More often than not, those who have these characteristics use them without expecting anything in return. In fact, they are so good at this that it seems like they were born with this attitude. However, people who are compassionate have chosen to live their lives this way. They understand that developing empathy toward others is an important part of life. This is a trait that all of us can put into practice immediately.

African Americans who have the IT factor have endless energy and enthusiasm. They are some of the most positive people we will ever meet. They are always moving forward and trying to help others get ahead. Their energy is contagious and they have no problem sharing their enthusiasm. It seems as if nothing gets them down. While this may or may not be the case, you would never know it. This is because they accentuate the positive even in the midst of their most difficult situations. If they are experiencing rough seas, they only share it with their inner circle that is in their lives for support. Positive people will not bring you down; instead, they tend to lift you up. This is a trait that we all can out into practice immediately.

To develop your IT factor, identify those people in your life that have it already and emulate their behaviors. As long as it is a genuine attempt, eventually you will develop the traits and characteristics of those who have the IT factor. Build your intelligence, show compassion, and remain positive. This is a good start to developing your IT factor. Continue to build it by helping others, being selfless, and making a commitment to excellence. These habits will become second-nature and soon you will be recognized as an attractive person who has the IT factor. At this point we should not be afraid to use what we have to improve our lives. Go ahead, you have earned IT!

Do you know any African Americans who have the IT factor?

Not everyone has IT. In fact, few people actually have IT.

If you have IT, use IT.

Self-Improvement

When you realize that you have IT, accept IT.

Do not be afraid to embrace IT.

Do not flaunt IT, because this is not necessary.

Everyone can see whether or not you have IT.

Most people will know if IT is real or an act.

If you don't have IT yet, understand that you can get IT.

So do not act like you have IT if you do not have IT.

Instead, build and develop IT.

Once IT is obtained, IT should be put into practice immediately.

IT cannot be taken away from you once you have IT.

Use IT for the right reasons.

Finally, teach others how to get IT.

As a final thought, careful observation of this analysis will show that I have not equated the IT factor to physical ability or appearance. That is not what this is about. This is about developing the traits and characteristics of successful African Americans. These people have qualities that cannot be measured. Instead, they have the intangibles that most people look to possess and put into practice. Once again, these traits can be learned and applied to our everyday lives and experiences. Once we develop our IT factor, we should let ourselves shine so that other African Americans will imitate our positive behaviors.

WAKE UP BLACK AMERICA! Do you have the IT factor?

WAKE UP! 42 Ways to Improve Black America NOW!

#24 Starve Yourself to Become Hungry

Being hungry is one of those God-given feelings that we should be most thankful to have. We all know what causes hunger: lack! If we lack eating enough food, we become hungry. If we lack the proper nutrients because we have not eaten properly, we will become hungry. The best part about hunger is that it forces us to want. When those hunger pains hit, we want to eat to end our hunger as soon as possible. Shortly thereafter, if we have not properly replenished our bodies what happens? We get hungry again!

Black America, we are not hungry anymore! Obviously this does not refer to eating, but it does refer to what we want. We have lost our edge; we have lost our desire to get better. We have lost our aspirations to improve our lot in society. In other words, we do not suffer from want. We are not starving to be successful. We are not hungry enough to demand improvements in ourselves, others, and our society. Why is it that African Americans are not as hungry as we used to be?

To answer this puzzling question, we can look back at our history in America. Already in this book, we have examined different times when black Americans faced hardships and difficulties to survive. These were the times when African Americans wanted more. For example, as slaves, blacks waited, prayed, and sometimes fought and died for freedom. We were hungry! Years later, many blacks lived with discrimination in communities and towns across America. Blacks protested, demonstrated, and sometimes fought and died for an end to segregation. We were hungry! In both cases, blacks wanted more. We wanted our share of the American dream.

As stated before, many of us think we have everything we need. To some, this means that there is no need to attain anything else. It allows African Americans to enter a comfort zone and harbor the unrealistic belief that we have made it. However, if you have lost a job and realized you were living paycheck to paycheck, you have not made it YET. If you

Self-Improvement

are reconsidering going back to school solely out of need thanks to the current financial crisis, you have not made it YET. If the current housing crisis forced you to downsize, sell, or face foreclosure, you have not made it YET. Starving yourself to get hungry once again is a way to turn "YET" into "YES".

Most of these situations happened because we were in a comfort zone and thought we had what we need. Personally, the comfort zone that I "enjoyed" was the safety net we call corporate America. Getting jobs has been easy, keeping them is easier, and earning a decent salary has never been a problem. But, there were two things that started making this comfort zone very uncomfortable. First, I realized if I were to lose my job tomorrow, I did not have a source of income that can sustain me for a few months until something else came along. Also, I learned the true definition of insanity (you will too before your finish this book). These two things made me hungry enough to pursue new opportunities.

To learn how to pursue new challenges, we must discuss what makes people hungry; not physically hungry, but mentally hungry. We look for a way to solve our physical hunger because we cannot tolerate our hunger pains any longer. WE TAKE ACTION by finding something to eat. We say to ourselves, enough is enough.

We must change something and change something quickly. On the other hand, changing our mental outlook is different. We tend to get mentally hungry once we receive a wake-up call about a given situation. It's a way to be reactive, not proactive. It also leads to inactivity until it is almost too late.

Now that we have come to the realization that we lack hunger, the next question to be answered is how African Americans can get hungry again? Simply put, WE MUST TAKE ACTION. We can no longer afford to wait or be reactive. While we wait, our people suffer. We must get out of the "comfort zone" of what we have. We should become hungry enough to want to change things, even if it looks like we have all we need. To solve our problems, black America must be more proactive.

WAKE UP! 42 Ways to Improve Black America NOW!

Instead of waiting for a wakeup call, WE MUST TAKE ACTION. We, as African Americans, must become so hungry that we are starved into taking action. This action must be done collectively, so that we can pool our resources and become powerful. We cannot allow situations to cool after our initial attempt to change things. What happened to the goals set during the Million Man March? Have we made an impact on police brutality? Will we make an impact on limiting the use of degrading language?

It is an amazing sight to see every time African Americans rally for a cause. We wield so much power that we are able to move insurmountable obstacles out of our way. This is a wonderful thing. However, one must ask why it takes us so long to take action. For example, gang violence, particularly in Los Angeles, was a local issue for years, waiting to explode in inner city neighborhoods across the country. It wasn't until media exposure via music, movies, and television exposed the extent of gang violence that we received our wake up call. By then, gang violence proliferated. Finally, we became hungry enough to take action in our attempts to combat gang violence.

A better way to deal with a problem such as increasing gang violence would have been to magnify the problem before it gained steam. We should have taken action to head off potential problems. We were in a comfort zone: our streets weren't that bad after all, were they? We were not hungry! Therefore, reality says that we must make our streets safer by being more proactive. Black Americans must understand that we cannot rely on anyone outside our community. No one can, or should, force us to become hungrier. It is up to us to change our lives.

WAKE UP BLACK AMERICA! Are your hungry yet?

Self-Improvement

#25 Write Down Your Goals & Action Plans

Everyone has goals! Goals can range from very small goals to extremely large goals. For example, a small goal could be trying to pass a test. A large goal could be trying to start a company. Regardless of the size of the goal, it is very important to prepare and plan if achieving it will become a reality. Contrary to popular belief throughout the course of our history in this country, African Americans have had goals too! In fact, many of our goals have become reality, thanks in large part to planning.

The best way to increase the odds of achieving a goal is to write it down. How many people write down goals? Statistics show that less than one out of every ten people writes down their goals! How does this translate into achievement? Chances are, this is the reason why two out of every ten people are living the lives they want. They are planning to work and working their plan. There is a direct relationship between writing goals and achieving them.

Writing down a goal by itself does not guarantee greater success. It only starts the process of achievement. Goals must be accompanied by action plans that clearly define how a goal will be reached. Action plans must include dates of completion for each step of the process of completing a goal. Without dates, there is no incentive or "pressure" to complete a given task. In other words, the hunger to complete a task is accompanied by setting specific deadlines.

Action plans must be broken down into steps. Each step, when added together, should equal completion of the goal. The steps should also have dates of completion. In other words, a goal will look like a blueprint or a series of instructions. Think about it: could you build a new house without a blueprint? Could you program the latest electronic device without step by step instructions? Without the blueprint or instructions, the likelihood of completing tasks is slim. It is also true when setting goals. Without a plan, the likelihood of completing them is slim.

WAKE UP! 42 Ways to Improve Black America NOW!

The goal-setting process also takes examination of potential obstacles that will surely come. Every goal, regardless of its scope, will be challenged. The goal of passing a test will be met by the challenges of what to study, when to study, and where to study. The goal of starting a business will be met by challenges of what industry to enter, what services to provide, and how to incorporate. In short, when you set a goal, problems will arise. The way to handle obstacles is to prepare for them.

Another list to consider is a list of obstacles that may or may not arise and solutions for each. This takes a lot of work, but doing this task increases your likelihood of success. After this exercise, dealing with potential challenges becomes easier. It also builds confidence when challenges that were anticipated arise and are handled thanks to planning. Momentum gained will help continue the march toward a goal despite the fact that new problems may occur. A prime example is Jackie Robinson, whose goal was to become a Major league baseball player. He prepared himself well in advance for setbacks and obstacles on his way to breaking the color barrier and becoming the first African American in Major League baseball.

If you were to take a survey in any given African-American community, one would find that many people believe that their dreams cannot become reality. Problems of all sorts stop momentum. This is because many people, especially in the black community, are conditioned to believe what they see. They stop themselves here, without exploring the possibilities of achieving goals. Doubt sets in, especially when those filled with doubt give faulty advice. The goal is put off. The dream dies a premature death.

Instead, African Americans should visualize what they want. The first method of visualization is a list of goals to accomplish. We should also surround ourselves with pictures of the things we want to accomplish. Pictures serve as powerful reminders of the thing we want. There is a saying: if you can see it, then you can be it!

Self-Improvement

Ask Dwight Howard, the National Basketball Association superstar who knows about setting goals and developing action plans. He, at an early age, wrote down his goals of being in the NBA and being the #1 draft pick. He posted these goals near his bed, in a place where he could see them every day. This became his springboard and motivation to work hard. In time, he developed as a player and was good enough to become the best high school player in America. On the night of the 2004 NBA draft, Dwight Howard came face to face with the law of attraction. He became the #1 draft pick and his goal of playing in the NBA became a reality.

Dwight Howard believes in the power of writing down goals. Do you? How many African Americans follow his example? How many African Americans write down their goals? How many African Americans would go on in spite of adversity? How many African Americans achieve their goals? This is what it takes to become successful. The highest of achievers in our race understand this. They know that success must be planned through setting and writing goals.

Here's a riddle that helps drive home the importance of setting goals: There were five cats sitting on a fence. 3 decided to jump. How many cats were sitting on the fence?

There were still 5 cats sitting on the fence. 3 DECIDED to jump but the riddle never says that they did!

African Americans could learn a lot from this riddle. Deciding to do something is not enough. We must take action! How do we start to take action? By setting goals, writing them down, setting time limits, and working hard until we are successful. This will defeat the idea that our dreams and goals are not attainable. They are! To borrow a line from President Obama: YES WE CAN!

WAKE UP BLACK AMERICA! Write down goals and action plans NOW!

#26 Stay the Course, Handle Adversity, and Control Your Destiny

Years ago, I met George Fraser, a famous African American author and motivational speaker. At a conference I was attending, he was the keynote speaker. George is an impressive man with an impressive set of credentials. Yet it was three short words that he used that left a lasting impression. After I purchased his book, I stood in line for him to sign it. I introduced myself to him, and he simply said three magic words: "stay the course." He also wrote this in my book. In fact, it is because of that single encounter that George Fraser has been my inspiration for writing this book and becoming a motivational speaker.

"Stay the course?" I didn't know it at the time, but now I understand what he was trying to say. During his keynote address, he spoke about being in control of your destiny. The main idea he was trying to make was to control your destiny by staying the course. Staying the course means not to give up, regardless of the circumstances or challenges that occur. Staying the course is another way of saying "hang in there."

Staying the course requires that we handle adversity associated with trying to achieve a goal. Adversity comes in many forms for African Americans. A prime example is prejudice and discrimination that still exists today. Both prevent us from getting jobs, houses, and other goods and services. In these cases, we must handle the adversity, and stay the course by finding the opportunities that will suit our needs. They do exist.

Another instance of handling adversity for black Americans is negative peer pressure and its consequences. Our children are under pressure to do things that their friends do just to fit in. As a result, many fall into the traps of gang violence and drug dealing. Both of these situations require the ability to handle adversity. They also require the ability to stay the course of not joining in this activity.

Self-Improvement

If we stay the course and handle adversity, then we can control your destiny. What is your destiny as an African American? I believe your destiny is to lead the world in the 21st century. Let's face it, the African American has survived more hardships and overcome many obstacles in America for a reason. That reason is to be an example to other peoples. Our destiny is in the future that we can build thanks to those who survived in our past.

Our opportunity lies in the fact that some black people do not know their course. We do not know our destiny. Since they are not aware of it, they do not understand that each of us has a role to play. Each African American must live life to the fullest. Each person must build and leave a legacy. Then, the collective power of our race will be on full display. We will finally take our place as the example for others to follow. You will complete your destiny!

Why should we stay the course? Why should we handle adversity? The answer is to fulfill our destiny! Anytime when we set a worthwhile, attainable goal, we should stay the course. Anytime we set a worthwhile goal, we should handle adversity. All of this will lead to controlling our future. We can no longer afford to leave things to others. We must take to command to achieve our destiny.

The history of black Americans is filled with stories of people who stayed the course and handled adversity for the benefit of our race and the entire world. They fulfilled their destiny! Booker T. Washington had no place to live so he slept outdoors while formulating his plans to educate black Americans. He fulfilled his destiny! Harriet Tubman was separated from her family, yet she found the courage to help others to freedom. She fulfilled her destiny! If they could stay the course and handle adversity, why can't we?

We have more advantages than any other generation of African Americans in the history of the United States. Therefore, we should be able to find solutions to any situation that presents itself. We need to simply set goals, plan, and work hard to achieve success. Then, we

WAKE UP! 42 Ways to Improve Black America NOW!

should pass on our success secrets to others so we can help rebuild our communities. Throughout this process, we must remember to stay the course. Throughout this process, we must remember to handle adversity. Then, we will be in control of our destiny. The time is now!

When is feels like everyone is against you… stay the course!

When life deals you a serious blow… stay the course!

When money is tight and your patience is thin… stay course!

When others say you can't get it done… stay the course!

When all else fails… stay the course!

WAKE UP BLACK AMERICA! Stay the course, handle adversity, and control our destiny!

Self-Improvement

#27 Accept Your Results and Do Something About Them

The most important way that African Americans can improve ourselves and our communities is to set goals, accept our results, and then try to improve on them going forward. If we set goals, write them down, address obstacles, work hard, and set dates of completion, there is no doubt in my mind that we can achieve every goal we set. However, most people choose to take shortcuts and ignore one or more of these steps. When people do not accomplish their goals, excuses are created to spread the blame for failures.

Excuses are monuments of nothing that build bridges to nowhere. Those who use these tools of incompetence are masters of nothingness.

An example in education comes to mind. As a teacher, report card time was always difficult. It was when I knew that some students would not be happy with the grades they would receive. I also knew that I would have my feelings hurt a few times once the grades came out. Some of my students blamed me for their grades!

A few classic lines thrown at me by dis-satisfied students:

"Why did you fail me?"
"Because of you, I have to go to summer school!"
"You didn't tell me I wasn't passing!"

What is the common thread throughout the three excuses? Each one of them puts the blame on the teacher. Yes things like this hurt my feelings, but not because of the words or accusations. It's because they didn't realize that they were in control. They had the final say in the grades the received. Instead of looking back to what they didn't do, they simply placed blame. They didn't accept their results. They also knew that they had no arguments against me. I was thorough with my grades and grading system. I followed the rules and went beyond what was expected of a teacher. I guess it felt good to blame someone!

The best way for students in this situation to remedy this situation is to accept their poor performance, find out how to improve it, and start to implement changes immediately. The students who used these excuses all had the same traits: they did not pay attention in class, they missed numerous homework assignments, and they missed a lot of school altogether! They could easily fix these three issues and improve their performance. They also had another trait: they were failing other classes as well.

We have a hard time accepting our results when they are poor. It's in our nature. We do not like criticism, and sometimes self-criticism is the hardest to take. Yet, it is how we learn, develop, and grow. The learning process is in full bloom when we make mistakes and figure out how to avoid the same mistakes the next time around. All inventions ever created followed this path. Thomas Edison performed over 1,000 experiments before he created the light bulb. Imagine if Edison would have accepted result 423 and stopped his experimentation. Yankee Candle might be the largest company in the world today!

The wonderful thing about human beings is that even if Edison stopped, someone else would have figured it out sooner or later. But this is not a reason to give up. As black Americans, this should be our rallying cry. Someone else will be born into better circumstances, don't give up. Someone else will have more education, don't give up. Someone else will have more possessions, don't give up. These are all temporary situations that have no bearing on our results.

As a matter of fact, these examples have nothing to do with us unless we allow them to influence our results. If we allow someone else's results to influence our attempts, then we can expect to come up short. A big part of success is to judge you against yourself. Did you give it your all when trying to complete a given task? We can learn how to accept our results if we learn how to look in the mirror and do some honest self-reflection and evaluation of our own actions.

Self-Improvement

We must learn how to accept our results and always IMPROVE upon them. Most people only think of improving when things go wrong. However, we must also improve when we have done our best! Sports are a great example of this concept. A baseball player steps to the plate and hits a sweet line drive for a hit. What does he want the next time he steps to the plate? At the least, he wants another hit; chances are he EXPECTS to hit a home run! A track and field runner sets a personal best mark in a race. What does she want the next time she lines up in the blocks? At the least, she wants another personal best; chances are she EXPECTS to set a new world record!

African Americans, your results are yours! Take ownership of them immediately. Then learn from the steps along the way that produced the results. What things need to change? What can be duplicated? Here is a mantra to live by: *I should be the first person to examine and critique my own results, both good and bad.* Besides, who really has time to worry about your results? We all have to worry about our own anyway.

This must be our mentality, regardless of whether we are at our very best or very worst. As black Americans, we should accept that we have citizens living below poverty level, and lift them out. We should also accept that we have citizens living in the middle class, and join them. Finally, we should accept that we have citizens living in the upper class, and duplicate their success. We can do it. All we need to do is start accepting our results and then plan to do something about them.

WAKE UP BLACK AMERICA! Accept your results and do something about them!

WAKE UP! 42 Ways to Improve Black America NOW!

#28 Keep Your Word/Honor Your Commitments

There are many times in our lives when all we have is our word. People listen intently and expect that we do what we say we will do. If we do not keep our word, then others view us as unreliable and undependable. Even worse than that, people learn not to trust those who do not keep their word. Now more than ever, African Americans need to feel that we can trust one another. Therefore, need to make sure we keep our word and honor our commitments to each other.

Keeping your word starts with thinking about what you say BEFORE you say it. Listening skills help a lot because we can tune in to what others say first. Once we understand what they want, then we can given the appropriate response. The response we give should be genuine and sincere. Also, African Americans should be committed to doing what it is that we say. In my opinion, the worse thing a person can do is tell you what they will do knowing that they have no intention of doing it.

A classic example comes to mind about the dating scene. Two people meet and spend awhile talking and getting to know each other. One or both parties realize that they would like to speak again in the future. However, this is when intentions come into play. If the man wants to communicate solely for hooking up, he will try to get a phone number for future use. Make no mistake about it, usually this is a game. He says he will call, but he will not commit to a specific time. He will only call IF the mood ever hits him. His intentions are not genuine. He did not keep his word.

On the other side of the encounter, the lady might see things entirely different. She might be interested so she would give her phone number. However, her expectations might only be that she will wait for a call but not expect one. She says call me, but life will go on if he does not. While this is a good strategy, giving a false phone number is not. If she does not

Self-Improvement

want to communicate after this meeting, her number could be (555) YOU-LOSE. In this case, even if it is warranted, her intentions are not genuine. She did not keep her word.

I believe that most people have a built in BS detector. We have it so that we can weed out those who we know will not keep their word. While it is true that many of us give each other the benefit of the doubt, we should not have to. We should expect that other African Americans will keep their word. In fact, we should demand it. We can easily make the short jump from being inconsiderate to boldface lying because someone does not keep their word. Once again, this does not lead to building trust.

Another thing that we should remember is that a part of keeping our word is honoring our commitments. Commitments are the next step after telling a person what we will do. When we say it, we commit to it. This is why many people will not give their "commitments" a specific date or time frame. However, making a commitment requires a time constraint. That puts the onus on us to keep our word and honor our commitments.

In the business world, honoring commitments can be the difference between success and failure for African Americans. Deadlines are a part of doing business so meeting them is extremely important. We should not make commitments in this arena unless we also commit to doing everything in our power to meet our deadlines. Many times, we miss deadlines at work due to various issues, but one of them should never be giving it less than 100% effort. We all know what missing too many deadlines in the workplace will lead: unemployment!

The business world is also filled with valuable networking opportunities for African Americans. We should take full advantage of working together with other people who have common goals. We can do this by phone, email, or face-to-face interaction. However, nothing can end a networking opportunity faster than failing to keep a commitment. A promise to make a contact that is not kept can void the trust and friendship that is built through networking. This is a lost opportunity that African Americans need to improve.

WAKE UP! 42 Ways to Improve Black America NOW!

The most important commitments that we make are to our families. These commitments are not to be taken lightly, because we make them to the most important people in our lives. Marriage is the most important commitment we will make in our lifetimes. Therefore, we must be ready when we enter into the commitment and we must intend on keeping it forever. Forever is a long time, so African Americans should think twice, and rehearse their wedding vows repeatedly before jumping the broom.

Our commitment to our children is just as important as our commitment to our marriages. Children take the commitments we make, or do not make, very seriously. It is important not to break these commitments to our children. Our commitments to them may be verbal, such as saying we will do something or be somewhere for them. Our commitments are also non-verbal, like doing whatever we can to insure they have what they need. In any event, having children means making a commitment to them. African Americans can ill-afford to break commitments to the children who need our guidance and support.

We must learn how to keep our word and honor our commitments so that we build trusting relationships. It is important that when we offer our word, we have the intention of living up to our commitment. These commitments can be on the dating scene, in the business world, or during daily interactions with friends and family. Regardless of the situation, our level of commitment must remain the same. As a result, we will experience more fulfilling personal and professional relationships.

WAKE UP BLACK AMERICA! Keep your word and honor your commitments.

Self-Improvement

COMMUNICATION IS A KEY TO WAKING UP BLACK AMERICA!
❖❖❖❖❖

We have established the importance of education, learned more about our story, become self motivated, and learned how to improve our lives. It becomes increasingly important that we share the knowledge we have. To share knowledge and experiences, we must be able to master all forms of communication. Far too often in the black community, our communication skills are not as good as they should be. This causes us to miss opportunities to grow and help others.

Communication encompasses many forms. We should be able to master spoken communication. We should be able to master written communication. We should be able to master non- verbal communication. We should also be vigilant and stand up against any form of communication that does not show African Americans in a good light. All of these things will allow us to use communication to tell a more positive story about our experiences as Americans.

29. Master the Written and Spoken English Language
30. Learn the Power of Words: Quotes
31. Learn a Second Language
32. You Are a Reflection on Your Race
33. Improve Your Body Language
34. Dress for Success
35. Stop Promoting Anger

Respect Our Story- Build Knowledge Through Education- Motivate Yourself- Look for Ways to Improve Yourself- Become a Master Communicator

… WAKE UP! 42 Ways to Improve Black America NOW!

#29 Master the Written and Spoken English Language

A vital component of the future of our race is how well we use the English language. Unfortunately we sometimes fail to see the importance of using our language properly. When we don't write or speak properly, it gives the impression that we are not intelligent. Obviously, those who are not intelligent do not get the same opportunities as an intelligent person. Therefore, it is important that we master the written and spoken English language, especially when we are young.

It really bothers me when African-American kids use slang as if it is the proper way to speak English. It transfers into their daily lives and follows them forever. I'll never forget the lady in my neighborhood who, with good intentions on getting her point across properly, asked the following question to her companion: "Is you coming back?" Being a teacher by trade, I wanted to correct her. Instead, I just looked. Of course, she had to repeat herself just to make sure she was heard: "Is you coming back?" Yes, she was African American.

She was probably in her thirties, so a logical assumption is that she had children. If so, what could they possibly learn from her about the correct way to speak English? Since she is their role model, they probably do not learn much from her. This is why we, as adults, must learn how to speak and write proper English. Our children can learn from us. The last thing we should want is for our children to learn in the street by repeating the language they hear.

Children also repeat the language they hear on television, radio, and in music. Slang dominates our culture and is thought of as "cool". So it makes sense, I suppose, that kids like to use it instead of proper English. It is important to note once again how some people in our race respond to black people who speak properly. If you use proper English, you are called a sellout, or you are thought to be acting white. What this

Self-Improvement

misguided thought process fails to realize is that language has no color; it is simply used properly or improperly. In fact, this line of thought will allow certain African Americans to keep bringing each other down.

Another concept that will keep black Americans down is the all but dead Ebonics movement. Ebonics was a concept based on the use of slang as an accepted way of speaking. This way, those who use slang could have an accepted language they can use INSTEAD of speaking Standard English. We all know who this pertained to: young, poorly educated black children. The problems with this were numerous. Did anyone think Ebonics would have been accepted at the workplace? No, therefore how would young people find employment? It was also a subtle way of saying that young African Americans were not smart enough to learn proper English, so let's "help" them out. Thanks but no thanks!

At this point we must not forget the written English language. We realize that slang is accepted on the streets, but do we know that it should rarely, if ever, be used in formal writing. In my teaching career, I have had to remind my students constantly of this fact. Yet, they continued to use slang in their writing. I had to use a scenario repeatedly to drive this point home.

In the example, I used a real cover letter that accompanied a resume for a job. In various versions of the letter, I had different characteristics. The first letter had obvious misspelled words. The second had poor sentence structure and grammatical errors. The third had no misspellings or errors, but was loaded with slang. The final letter was perfect. The students were required to read and correct each of the first three letters. After this, they were to read the correct version. In the final analysis, the students would be asked which letter should warrant a job interview. Naturally, all agreed that the perfect letter was the best.

After an exercise like this, I always thought I had them. Then they would start writing again, still using slang in their research papers as if they were talking to their friends! They couldn't, or didn't want to, grasp the concept of writing as a way to properly express ideas. They didn't

WAKE UP! 42 Ways to Improve Black America NOW!

understand the perception that their writing gives a snapshot of their intelligence. People, especially those in positions of power, hold proper written communications in the same high regard as spoken communication. Once again, those who can write proper English are held in higher esteem than those who write poorly.

Using spoken and written English correctly revolves around our self-esteem. The connection to using proper English is obvious, yet the connection it has to the way we feel about ourselves isn't. There is no excuse for using poor English, especially when our school systems emphasize it. However, any subject becomes more difficult if the learner's self-esteem prevents them from thinking they can do things correctly. We must break this. Students should know that learning proper English is not too difficult. Also, it will lead to greater successes academically and socially. It does not lead to trying to be white; it leads to trying to be successful.

WAKE UP BLACK AMERICA! Learn the written and spoken English language!

Self-Improvement

#30 Learn the Power of Words and Quotes

As a high school senior, many students are asked to give a quote that sums up their personality for everyone to remember them by. I was assigned this task and it took days for me to select the perfect quote. After checking out hundreds of sayings, I finally decided to use my own. I said this quote to myself, never uttering it for someone else to hear. Under my picture in the St. Aloysius High School 1989 yearbook, it reads:

"Get loose and produce!"

It was catchy; it was mine. However, there was a big problem with selecting this quote on two fronts. The first problem was that the yearbook editor and staff refused to print it until I provided some clarification. The quote could have a sexual connotation, so they wanted me to explain it further. I told them it was about stepping up and achieving goals. They bought it. Besides, I'll admit that I wasn't the ladies' man I could have been in high school anyway, so the dirty side of the quote never entered my mind.

There was a second problem. I didn't believe in my own quote! I didn't put it into practice as much as I should have. I didn't get loose and produce! Instead, I got tight and barely produced, not nearly as much as I knew I should have. An amazing thing happened to me when I saw my quote in print in the yearbook. I realized that it had power. It had meaning. It was a reflection of me. And, it was a lie! From that realization, I learned the power of using quotes.

While attending college, I had a collection of my favorite quotes plastered on my dorm room walls. The quotes provided me with motivation and courage under fire. For me, the quotes were fun to collect. There are good quotes about every situation and problem that can provide courage, strength, wisdom, and guidance. By far, the one place

WAKE UP! 42 Ways to Improve Black America NOW!

where the most, and best quotes can be found is in the Bible. The Book of Proverbs is a great source of these precious gems.

As African Americans, some of us need all of the help we can get when dealing with the hardships of everyday life. Quotes can help us; especially quotes from other black Americans who used them to their advantage. Where can we find quotes from black Americans? Thousands of books written by black Americans, for black Americans, and about black Americans provide all of the quotes we need. Once again, we can duplicate the things that successful people used to repeat and build upon their achievements.

The following list is random quotes from various sources on various topics. Some of them have become personal mantras that I use in everyday situations. They are free and can be used repeatedly to suit our needs. Half of the quotes are attributed to African Americans. Whenever the original author of a quote could not be found but it has relevance to our situation, it is attributed to an anonymous source...

-Very early in life I became fascinated with the wonders language can achieve. And I began playing with words. -Gwendolyn Brooks

-Nothing ventured, nothing gained.-Anonymous

-There is in this world no such force as the force of a person determined to rise. The human soul cannot be permanently chained. -W.E.B. DuBois

-The capacity to believe is what you receive.-Anonymous

-From the first, I made my learning, what little it was, useful every way I could.-Mary McLeod Bethune

-Some people dream of success while others stay awake and work hard at it. -Anonymous

- Humor is laughing at what you haven't got when you ought to have it.

112

Self-Improvement

-Langston Hughes

-Successful people do what critics say can't be done. -Anonymous

-Education is for improving the lives of others and for leaving your community and world better than you found it. -Marian Wright Edelman

-Fortune favors the bold. -Anonymous

-I prefer to be true to myself, even at the hazard of incurring the ridicule of others, rather than to be false, and to incur my own abhorrence. -Frederick Douglass

-Get loose and produce. -Gary McAbee

WAKE UP BLACK AMERICA! Learn the power of using quotes!

WAKE UP! 42 Ways to Improve Black America NOW!

#31 Learn a Second Language

Learning proper English is not enough. In today's shrinking global economy, learning how to communicate with people of other races is crucial. It is also an aspect that few African Americans take full advantage of. If we could effectively communicate in different languages, we can open up new doors to commerce, investments, and knowledge. We need to find every competitive advantage that we can, and being bilingual is definitely one that we can use.

Throughout our formal education, we have been wrapped in a comfort zone of only having to learn English. During the process, the concept of learning our language has been hammered home with mixed results. For those of us who are good at using the English language, doors open and opportunities abound. For others who struggle with the language, difficulties lie ahead. This is why it is only after mastering English that we should tackle a second language. Usually, by the time we are ready to tackle another language during our formal education, we have already had enough exposure to English.

In America, the obvious choice for learning a second language is Spanish. A comparison between English-speaking and Spanish-speaking children in the US is an interesting contrast. Our children only learn English; meanwhile, their children learn Spanish, but must also learn English because they are in an English-speaking country. It gives them a distinct advantage over our children when it comes to language. They are put through the process of learning a formal language twice. Their exposure to both languages will be helpful in the future as the need for both languages coexists.

It has been said that Americans who speak Spanish will be in the majority by the year 2060. This means that African Americans should take advantage of this by learning Spanish. In fact, it will make communication a lot easier for us in the future. It will also help us now. In major cities throughout the US, there are large pockets of Spanish-

Self-Improvement

speaking people in various neighborhoods. This spurs the need for people who can speak Spanish, as well as English, to provide services to this growing segment of our communities.

I am a witness to how important it is to learn Spanish. My family relocated from Pittsburgh to Toledo, Ohio. In both places, the need to know Spanish wasn't pressing because both cities have relatively small Spanish populations. However, when we relocated again to New Jersey, everything changed because of the large Spanish- speaking population. Services for Spanish-speaking people were numerous, and they needed workers who can speak both English and Spanish. A lot of those opportunities were wide open for those who were bilingual, yet many of those opportunities remained open for months, because a lot of people aren't bilingual.

Recently, there has been a backlash that says that English is the official language so everyone should speak it exclusively. The real issue is whether Spanish should become a second official language in the United States. This is in relation to the illegal immigration and status of many inhabitants of our country. While I don't encourage Spanish as a second official language, I do encourage it as an "unofficial" one. The fact is that any idea that limits learning of a different language naturally goes against the idea of more education for our people.

Spanish is not the only language that is good to learn. Japanese is becoming more and more popular in higher education. Japanese is good to know because of the expanding impact of Japan's economy. African Americans could use Japanese to open doors to this growing market. I recall reading an article about a black woman executive who was fluent in Japanese. Let's face it; a black woman who speaks Japanese would surely open doors! Yes, she is highly successful and makes multi-million dollar deals with Japanese firms. This is a perfect example of taking advantage of a second language to compete and win in the global marketplace.

Learning a second, or multiple languages, is not only important for being

WAKE UP! 42 Ways to Improve Black America NOW!

competitive in today's global marketplace. We should learn new languages for the sake of learning. In particular, the languages that we should want to know more about are the hundreds of dialects used in Africa. Some critics of the Motherland would say that even today, Africa is not as developed as other parts of the world. However, when looking at language, it is amazing to have such an erroneous belief when considering the amount of different tongues used in Africa throughout history.

Swahili is a language that I recall being learned by students in colleges across the country. The impressive thing about this is that it is a subject that is usually taken for the sake of learning. We know this because it is not a language African Americans need to know to be successful in our country today. Therefore, learning Swahili has to be viewed as either curiosity or making a connection to our people in Africa.

Swahili is used today in children's names such as Khadijah, Aaliyah, and Fatima. This is proof that there is an interest in the language and the meanings of its words. For example, the singer Aaliyah was one of our brightest stars, so it is fitting that her means one of the highest, or on a high level in Swahili. Obama is a word that means "to lean" or "be uncertain". Although his name may mean uncertainty, we know our President to be certain about the issues! The fact remains that the meanings of words and names can build interest in languages such as Swahili.

As a final thought, learning different languages will go a long way in helping to solve today's problems and meet tomorrow's challenges in our world. Breaking down barriers such as language can bring people closer together and show that we are more similar than we realize. African Americans have a huge part to play in this as well. We have a role in improving relations around the world, and learning different languages can help in this mission.

WAKE UP BLACK AMERICA! Knowing two languages is better than one!

Self-Improvement

#32 You Are a Reflection of Your Race

Many of our people ignore the fact that each of us is a reflection on our entire race. If one of us speaks broken English, it is a poor reflection on all of us. If one of us acts inappropriately in public, it is a reflection on all of us. This is why we must improve the way we speak and act in public. Not only should we do this for ourselves, we should do it for each other. Most importantly, we should speak and act properly so that our children and teenagers learn from us.

Our young people take cues from us. Therefore, it is easy to see why some of our children act the way they do. They have not been taught the right way to speak and act. In fact, they tend to learn from poor examples of how to behave. They emulate these behaviors as a result. For the most part, the behavior of many black children can be traced to the way the adults in their lives act. If the adults do not know how to behave, chances are the children will not know either.

Aren't you tired of watching one of our children misbehaving in school and in the neighborhood? Aren't you tired of adults acting "ghetto" in the streets? Aren't you tired of loud black people? Aren't you tired of rude adults and children who seem to lack concern for others? Aren't you tired of black people who do not act properly in public?

An example of poor behavior illustrates the frustration of many black people. Recently I needed to ride the train to get from point A to point B. On this day, service was interrupted; so many people were waiting a long time. Needless to say, people were upset. When the train arrived, it quickly became overcrowded with people. Those who were still trying to board had to squeeze their way through the doors of the cramped train. An older, white gentleman with two suitcases barely made it in before the doors closed.

Inadvertently, one of his suitcases hit me. I didn't mind because we were packed in, shoulder to shoulder. Then, he hit someone else, a young,

WAKE UP! 42 Ways to Improve Black America NOW!

black female. She immediately went off. Not only did she curse at him, but she gave him a shove in the back! This caused him to bump into others, nearly creating an avalanche of bodies. The young lady continued her loud verbal tirade, complete with broken English and many curses.

At this point, I need to inject race into this example. If you have ever been to the New York City metropolitan area, you would know that many races of people could be found on any given subway car at any given time. This was the case; I noticed because I looked around to see who was paying attention to this episode. Everyone was! Then I noticed something else. For some unexplained reason, black people on the train looked at each other. I did it too. All of us had the same look in our eyes and had the same thought: another, young, ignorant, black person, who doesn't know how to speak and act properly in public, has embarrassed all of us once again.

Notice how race plays a factor in this situation. A black woman overreacted and created a problem. Other black people lamented the fact that we look bad once again. I am 100% sure that people from other races observed, and quietly reaffirmed their beliefs about some African Americans. The bottom line is: we wonder why many people outside of the black race have such a negative view of us. We also wonder why there is a disconnection between older, more mature black people, and the younger generation. It is because some black folks don't know how to speak and act properly!

There are a number of ways to fix this problem. The first way is to understand that no one lives a life isolated from others; the actions of each of us will have some effect on someone else. Having consideration for others is a key to improving behavior. If the things we do or say could have a negative impact on someone else, then we should think twice before doing them. For example, cursing at a child might cause that child to start cursing too. This is not what any reasonable person would want.

Another thing that can be done to improve the way we speak and act in

Self-Improvement

public is to think positively. The effects of this can only lead to improved behavior. If we were to think about it, being positive will lead to less reliance on using negative words, such as curses. Also, people who try to be more positive will lead to less reliance on negative actions, such as fighting.

Finally, the educated masses of African Americans should become better mentors and role models in our communities. We all share the responsibility of helping our fellow citizens to correct their behavior. Our children need adults who model speaking proper English and good behavioral skills. This behavior must also be modeled in our schools and communities. When we learn to speak and act properly, we will have the power to influence massive changes in our lives.

WAKE UP BLACK AMERICA! Let's remember that we represent our entire race!

WAKE UP! 42 Ways to Improve Black America NOW!

#33 Improve Your Body Language

Every African American must master the subtle art of improving our body language to promote a better image in our society. Body language speaks volumes about how a person is feeling, their outlook on life, and how they conduct their business. A concept directly related to body language is making a first impression. First impressions are extremely important; those who leave good impressions will be more likely to achieve success than those who do not.

An example of this is a scene I witnessed at a local employment agency. Both inside and outside, a crowd of 15-20 men gathered every day to look for blue collar jobs. Most of them were not well spoken, so the impressions they gave were probably not conducive to getting employment. Even worse, their body language painted a bleak outlook and made it hard for them to be considered for employment. When looking at these men, it was clear that their body language had to leave a poor impression on the workers at the agency.

In front of the agency, some of the black men talked openly about their search for a job. They presented very poor body language; therefore, they found it hard to get a job. All of them had poor posture. All of them had nervous energy. All of them had frowns on their faces. As they continued their tirade, a well dressed, African American college instructor confidently walked by. So what was the difference between them and me? For starters, my appearance and body language painted a picture of success.

How could these men increase their chances of landing a job at the agency? They could have improved their body language to set themselves apart from the rest. Unfortunately, no one takes the time to teach these vital skills. The fact that many black people have never been schooled on the concept of body language makes it somewhat understandable if they give off poor impressions. However, no one cares

Self-Improvement

if we have not been taught proper social skills. We will continue to be passed over and dismissed instead of being taken seriously.

There are many skills that will improve our body language. When combining proper body language with using proper English and dressing for success, there is no doubt that African Americans can compete, and win in any situation. We simply need to master the skills that so many high achievers use to guarantee their success. The following skills are keys to improving our body language.

Demonstrate Good Posture

We should stand up straight and hold our head high. When sitting, we should lean slightly forward and be sure to be upright without slouching. These actions show confidence. They present a positive outlook and give off a good first impression.

Maintain Proper Eye Contact

Those who make good eye contact are perceived as trustworthy. We should learn how to look others directly in the eye when speaking. This is especially important when we are trying to make a favorable impression.

Give a Firm Handshake

A firm handshake shows confidence. It also shows strength and eagerness. Those who give firm handshakes are taken seriously and they are well respected.

Use Proper Hand Gestures

Hand gestures suggest excitement and energy. When speaking, use proper hand gestures to make points clear and emphasize ideas. Be careful not to constantly move the hands because it portrays nervousness. Use hand movements that come naturally; do not force them.

WAKE UP! 42 Ways to Improve Black America NOW!

Add Appropriate Responses

When engaged in conversations, use appropriate responses that include both verbal and non-verbal reactions. Such reactions include appropriate facial expressions, short pauses before speaking, and verbal responses to show that you are listening. Proper responses lead to more meaningful conversations.

Don't Forget to Smile

A smile works regardless of the situation at hand. It disarms people and gives the most positive response. Those who smile often are more likely to demonstrate their positive outlook. People tend to respond favorably to people who smile.

Each of these concepts will allow us to give off the correct body language and make better impressions. African Americans should put these things into practice immediately. They could be the difference between opening doors to new opportunities or closing doors to lost opportunities.

It is shameful that the men at the employment agency did not use these traits. Chances are that they will constantly struggle to find opportunities. They will have a hard time understanding why they are being passed by. And of course, they will be standing on the outside looking in when trying to find a job. When will we learn to clean up our speech, knowledge, and body language before we can achieve success?

WAKE UP BLACK AMERICA! Improve your body language today!

Self-Improvement

#34 Dress for Success

Thinking back, I remember when I was driving through Wilmington, NC when I heard on the radio that a famous black comedian had some poignant words about black America during the commemoration of the Brown vs. Board of Education ruling. Bill Cosby let his feelings be known about the state of our African American children. One important aspect he discussed was the way our children dress and present themselves in public. To paraphrase Mr. Cosby, he said that the way our children dress is an embarrassment to our race.

In my opinion, his words were right on target. However, many people didn't agree with him. They felt that he was too hard on black children and their parents. As in many circles, there is an unwritten rule in our community that says you should not air your dirty laundry in public. And yet, Bill Cosby aired enough dirty laundry to fill your local Suds-O-Rama! Many people criticized him for his views and the way he presented them, but Black America should be thankful.

We should be thankful because Mr. Cosby spoke out, and he told the truth. Some of our children dress as if they think they have no future. They do not fit in with the standards of dress that our society associates with being intelligent. Bill Cosby understands this; it is why he chose to speak out. The point he was trying to make is that our kids are already in the public eye, so everyone already sees how they dress. Their clothing is shameful, tacky, and in most cases, not age appropriate.

What is the cause for our children dressing they way they do?

Many people will blame the entertainment industry. If a rapper wears baggy jeans hanging off his backside, it must be alright! If video vixens wear tight-fitting, flesh-revealing outfits it must be alright! Honestly, dressing like this might pass in the world of music videos, but it should not carry over to everyday life.

WAKE UP! 42 Ways to Improve Black America NOW!

Reality is that kids see adults dress inappropriately so they think it's alright. They imitate what they see, so the question to be asked is: "Who is really at fault?" Also, one should wonder how they are allowed to imitate dressing inappropriately. It is because an adult allows them to. In fact, the adult often encourages it. Adults either buy the clothing their children wear or give them money for them to buy on their own. Then, dressing inappropriately is further encouraged when parents do not know what their children wear on a day-to-day basis with the money the adult provides. They don't take the time to find out.

We need to understand that many experiences in life are based on our appearance. How we dress is very important. It says a lot about our personality and outlook on life. A person who dresses in professional attire looks the part of being professional. This can open a lot of doors and become an advantage. On the other hand, a person who dresses "street" looks the part of being "street." This also opens doors and becomes and advantage, in the streets!

Some people will say that clothes do not make a person. While it is true that clothes do not make the person, they do give a strong impression. Others will say that you can't judge a book by its cover. This is also true, but the way the cover looks is very important. Finally, people will say that they are free to do whatever they want. Well we are free, but our actions still have an effect on others. In other words, even though all of these ideas are valid, dressing inappropriately will have a strong impression on others.

Why should we, as a community, improve our way of dressing? The reason is to build confidence, courage, and portray a successful look. A big part of dressing for success is not being afraid to stand out from the crowd. Many people, especially in the black community, conform and dress like everyone else in their inner circle. This becomes a problem if their inner circle has a thug mentality, or a "ghetto fabulous" mentality. Everyone looks the same, and they are all labeled as unwilling, or unable to succeed.

Self-Improvement

Instead, we should dress to promote where we want to go in life. Let's face the facts; although I do not favor conformity, this is one area where we should try to conform. We should imitate the way successful people dress, regardless of their race. This is the type of imitation that can have positive, long lasting effects. A person who dresses for success is more likely to exude the confidence that breeds success.

Dr. Cosby said it best: putting clothes on backwards should be a sign that something is wrong. To build on his point, putting on jeans that hang below the waist is a sign that something is definitely wrong. The sign is the thug culture that has infested our neighborhoods. Wearing skirts and jeans that show off the underwear is a sign that something is wrong. The sign is the "ghetto fabulous" culture that has infested our neighborhoods. The signs are there, black America. When will we pay attention?

WAKE UP BLACK AMERICA! Dress for success, not for the street!

WAKE UP! 42 Ways to Improve Black America NOW!

#35 Stop Promoting Anger

Our children are angry! We can tell that they are angry by the way they walk, talk, and conduct themselves. This is why many African American kids are rebellious, hard-headed, and stubborn. They are ready to fight any time someone slights them. They have built up anger that boils over. For example, sometimes stepping on a kid's sneaker is an offense punishable by death! Where have we gone wrong?

Let's take this a step further. Now we communicate anger with the clothes we wear. Remember the lovable Looney Tunes? Bugs Bunny, Taz, Tweety, and the gang represented hours of laughs and good times. Now they represent "thug life?" Our young people started wearing t-shirts that depicted the Looney Tunes doing all sorts of wild behavior. Taz was smoking cigarettes, or was that weed? Bugs Bunny had a bandana on his head! Tweety had a pistol! And all of them had an angry, "get out of my way or I'll slap you" look about them. Bugs, Tweety and Taz are gangsters! What is this world coming to?

So, I can understand, but not condone, the behavior of our young people. All they see is violence, anger, and frustration in the black community. All they see is violence on television and in video games. All they hear is the "get rich or die trying'" messages in music and the media. Therefore, they act out what they see. The question is: where does this anger come from?

The answer is obvious! Our children's anger comes from us, the adults of the African American community. We promote anger; we communicate anger. Our children are watching. They are watching our every move. Not only do they pick up on our actions, they also imitate them. So, if a parent or other "role model" promotes an angry, "me against the world" attitude, then their children will do the same.

What happens when a child or teenager displays their anger? We all know who is first to experience a challenge by an angry child: the parent

Self-Improvement

or guardian. After this the next victim will be a sibling, friend, or classmate. As this anger grows, eventually it will be used against people in authority. Teachers and other adult authority figures know how difficult it is to deal with someone else's angry child.

At this point, most adults will blame the outside world for their child's behavior. Yet, when examining the evidence, it becomes clear that anger is being communicated constantly in our homes. It is being communicated constantly in our schools. It is being communicated constantly in our neighborhoods. As a result, the by-product of this anger plays out in African- American communities across our nation.

What amazes me is the fact that most of us don't even know what we are angry about. Think about it; what are we upset about? Most African Americans enjoy a lifestyle that our ancestors could not even dream about. In fact, we have surpassed their expectations already. We have proven that we can be productive members of society. We have also proven that we can overcome any obstacles put in our way. An honest assessment would show that our anger comes from not being as successful as we want to be.

The solution to this problem is for black Americans to become more successful so that we can stop promoting anger. We waste far too much time being angry. Instead, we should get over ourselves and seek positive results. We must teach our children to seek positive results. The following list contains a few strategies to avoid promoting anger and frustration in our lives…

In the household:

-Keep adult situations between adults. In other words, arguments, frustrations, financial issues and other problems should be dealt with privately. Do not involve children.

-Talk to children about the negative, violent images they see and hear. Counter these influences with positive examples and images.

WAKE UP! 42 Ways to Improve Black America NOW!

In the neighborhood:

-Explain to children about the environment they live in. Show them how they can avoid being caught up in a cycle of violence.

-Give examples of education and learning at work in the community. Provide role models beside yourself for them to emulate.

In general:

-Speak positively around children. Smile. Give them safe places to play and develop. Remove any negative influences out of their lives whenever it's possible.

-Allow children to build the same skills illustrated in this book. Let them practice trial and error, then correcting mistakes while they are young. Prepare them for a bright future.

The truth of the matter is that success is a few steps away, if we can concentrate our efforts on getting to work on making improvements. Now that we know this fact, we should face our future with a more positive outlook. This reduces negative thinking thereby reducing our anger. African Americans who reduce their anger will not promote anger or negative images. This is why the concepts go hand in hand. When we stop promoting anger, we will become a more positive reflection on our race.

WAKE UP BLACK AMERICA! Stop promoting anger!

SUPPORT: A KEY TO WAKING UP BLACK AMERICA!
❖❖❖❖❖❖

Now that we have learned more about our story, established the need for education, become self motivated, formulated plans for self improvement, and figured out the importance of communication, we must provide support to each other. It does little good if one of us achieves success and leaves the rest behind without sharing experiences, knowledge, and a blueprint for others to follow. Therefore, we must offer support to help each other and fix our problems.

Support comes in many forms. We can offer support by giving our blessings and help when someone needs it. We can give advice if we have enough experience to give a proper judgment. We can be more positive, and associate ourselves with positive people. Most importantly, we can be more enthusiastic in our daily lives. All of these things provide support that others may need to become successful.

36. Be a Stereotype Breaker
37. Avoid Spreading Negative Energy
38. Don't be a Dream Stealer
39. Give Advice Under Two Conditions
40. Don't Mess With My Code of Ethics
41. Choose a Positive Role Model
42. Surround Yourself With Positive People

Respect Our Story- Build Knowledge Through Education- Motivate Yourself -Look for Ways to Improve Yourself- Become a Master Communicator- Support Each Other

WAKE UP! 42 Ways to Improve Black America NOW!

#36 Be a Stereotype Breaker

African Americans are fully aware of the stereotypes that have been used to define our race for many years. Some stereotypes are silly and do not deserve our attention. For example, who cares if black people are associated with eating fried chicken and watermelon? We do and we enjoy them both. Who cares if we are stereotyped as terrific athletes? We are great athletes and we love to hit the court and "ball." These stereotypes are harmless. However, other stereotypes can cause damage that is difficult to repair, especially when the stereotype is negative and we live up to it.

There are many negative stereotypes that serve as poor reflections on our race. The first of these stereotypes is that black men are not responsible fathers so we have poor family structures. Nothing can be farther from the truth. There are many black men who are handling the daily responsibilities of being a father. These African American men are also good husbands and role models for their children. Unfortunately, men like this don't get their due or the respect they deserve. As a result, the stereotype of black men who do not take care of their families lives on. To break the stereotype of being disinterested fathers, more African American men must step up and handle their responsibilities.

Another stereotype that is widely accepted is that black women are not good mothers to our children. Nothing can be farther from the truth. African American women have shown their resilience as mothers and fathers in many situations. While many may see their responses to these situations as carrying an attitude, one must look at the hardships our women have endured to appreciate their struggles. To break the stereotype of being unfit mothers, black women must continue to be the strength and backbone of our people.

Many people think that African Americans are more likely to be violent the people of other races. Nothing can be farther from the truth. There are numerous black people that are incarcerated for committing violent crime. Yet the amount of us that do not engage in violent activity is far greater. On any given Sunday, visit any African American church and you will see hundreds of law abiding, God-fearing people. The overwhelming majority of these people would go out of their way to help before they would consider causing harm to others. To break the stereotype of being prone to violence, we must make better choices and solve our disputes rationally.

For many years, a belief has been that African Americans are not able to be educated like people of other races. Nothing can be farther from the truth. Our people are improving in classrooms from grade school all the way to the college level. We are attending colleges and earning four year degrees. Some of us are getting our advanced degrees as well. While we do have a long way to go concerning the education of our people, it is laughable to say that African Americans are not capable of performing well academically. To break the stereotype of being uneducated, we must continue to emphasize the pursuit of knowledge.

Our people have been stereotyped as a race of lazy people who do not want to work. Nothing can be farther from the truth. We have worked since the first day that our ancestors reached these shores in the 1700s. We have been involved in the building of this country and its growth and development. We have been faithful employees in thousands of companies and American institutions. In the future, African Americans will work and contribute to the America of the future. To break the stereotype of not wanting to work, we must involve all of our people in the task of rebuilding our communities.

African Americans who successfully hold jobs, climb the corporate ladder, and attend various universities are stereotyped as being the recipients of Affirmative Action. Affirmative Action is one of the most misunderstood concepts that affect African Americans. It was set up to level the playing field, not give us jobs over more qualified applicants. In the past we did not get opportunities at all. Now we get a chance to compete. Even though we can now compete, it does not mean that we are given anything. In fact, we still have to earn everything we get. We are

WAKE UP! 42 Ways to Improve Black America NOW!

moving up the corporate ladder slowly, but surely, based not on any racially based quota system. To break the stereotype of being unqualified for the openings we get, we must improve our education and readiness for all opportunities.

Stereotypes have proven to cause damage to African Americans. Therefore, we should be keenly aware of the power that they possess. Because of this knowledge, we should not use stereotypes against another race of people. We are way beyond that. We should not use stereotypes to classify others, nor use them to hinder their progress. The truth of the matter is that no one appreciates being stereotyped. Stereotyping also goes beyond racial lines. We should not stereotype based on social status, sexual orientation, or religious beliefs.

African Americans must become stereotype breakers! By doing so, we will eliminate yet another unseen hurdle that is designed to hinder our progress. It will also improve relations between the races. It will also prevent situations in which people are judged unfairly. If people would avoid buying into ridiculous stereotypes, then they would have to work on getting to other each other. We need more of this behavior and less reliance on believing inaccurate stereotypes of African American people.

WAKE UP BLACK AMERICA! Break all stereotypes!

Support

#37 Avoid Spreading Negative Energy

The world we live in is full of negative energy. All it takes to realize this fact is to watch the eleven o'clock news in any major city. The top story is usually about an act of violence or another neighborhood tragedy. Unfortunately, far too many of these events occur in the black community. This vicious cycle of negative energy lives and breathes in our community.

Obviously, people are responsible for their attitudes and behaviors. So the "easy" solution is to stop being negative; instead, be positive! Of course, this is easier said than done, especially when many African Americans possess a bleak outlook on their future. Therefore, the only way too curb our negative tendencies is to start by being able to recognize them before we communicate them.

Think about it for a few seconds: how many people know when they are being negative? How many people know when they are spreading their negative thoughts and energy? Most negative thinkers tend to be so gloomy that they can not distinguish when they are being pessimistic. It is so deeply entrenched in their daily routines that it is second nature. An example of a person who fits this category is the constant complainer.

My rule of thumb to recognize when we promote negative energy is to ask a simple question: did the receiver of my message ask or expect me to give negative response? To examine this, observe the following two people locked in a conversation. Notice how one person will espouse negative responses while the other is "forced" to react to them. The reaction will determine how far the gloomy conversation will go…

The messenger: "I can't wait until its time to leave, this is really boring!"

The responder: "Me too, I have better things to do with my time."

The messenger: "What a waste of time. I'll never do this again!"

133

WAKE UP! 42 Ways to Improve Black America NOW!

In this short exchange, the messenger brought out a reply by introducing a negative idea. In turn, the responder chimed right in, continuing the pessimistic conversation. We all know that this could go on for minutes or in most workplaces for hours, with both parties singing the blues and sharing their misery. We also know what will happen if a third negative person enters the conversation… more drama!

What would happen if the responder had a different reply…

The messenger: "I can't wait until its time to leave, this is really boring!"

The responder: "Maybe so, but hang in there. I'm sure we can learn something from this."

Would the next thing the messenger says be stronger or weaker? The responder had to "disarm" the messenger with a little optimism. This is called putting a positive spin on a situation. It's the "look on the bright side" response. It takes away from the pessimistic tone of the conversation and disarms the messenger. But why should we have to be disarmed of our negativity? Why put someone else in that position? We should learn how to control it ourselves when we communicate.

Let's face facts; everyone has a reason to complain. We all have our crosses to bear. So why is it that most people expect you to carry your cross and theirs? Perhaps subconsciously, this is exactly what the negative person wants, to bring you down on their level. Maybe it's a way to feel better about a situation…"let me get this off my chest." Great, now I feel better and you feel worse! Thank you for sharing in my misery! I have just spread my negative energy to you, as if you didn't have enough troubles of your own.

In the African-American community, spreading negative energy takes many forms. Yes there is a "lack" of jobs, but we can complicate it by discouraging someone else from looking. Yes some of our schools are failing, but we can complicate it by discouraging those who are trying to

Support

succeed anyway. Yes our communities are ravaged by violence, but we can complicate it by labeling our youth as misguided. Yes our lives many not be perfect, but we can complicate them by letting everyone else see and hear about it too.

As African Americans, we should find a select few people who are WILLING to listen to our problems. These people become our supporters and helpers when we are in need. They actually want to hear our problems and offer support. They want to deflect our negative energy or turn it into something positive. Usually, these people are a spouse, parent, or best friend. They allow us to contain our negative energy without spreading it to others, especially to others who don't need the extra burden.

We should try with all our might to recognize when our negativity spills over and has an impact on someone else. In fact, let's back up. We should realize our negativity is about to spill out, and then prevent it from having an impact on someone else. I heard an expression that speaks to the concept of avoiding the spread of negative energy: Build a bridge and get over it! Notice that the expression isn't: Build a bridge and get over it, but only after you have pushed someone else off first.

WAKE UP BLACK AMERICA! Avoid spreading your negative energy, its contagious!

#38 Don't Be a Dream Stealer

A friend comes to you and tells you about their dream to start a restaurant. She is very excited, and she is able to give plenty of details about her plans for the venture. To you, it seems like a good idea, but it is very difficult to start and keep a restaurant in business. In fact, statistics show that 9 out of every 10 new restaurants fail. As she continues, you start to form your opinion. After she finishes talking, she anxiously waits for your reply to this question: "so what do you think?"

My African American friends, your first reaction will speak volumes about your true feelings about what you have heard. It is a nonverbal response that you send based on what you are hearing, also known as body language. It gives an immediate response, usually before you say anything. What body language do you think you would give if a friend told you they wanted to open a restaurant?

If the answer is a blank stare, smirk, rolling of the eyes, losing eye contact, or any other negative response, you might be a dream stealer! Who is a dream stealer? A dream stealer is a person who finds a reason to rob someone else of their dream. The dream stealer uses body language to take away a dream first. Perhaps, the dream stealer doesn't realize they have sent a negative response with their body language. Therefore, they must send a stronger response verbally.

In the restaurant situation, you might say to your friend...

"Have you given this ANY thought?"

"What makes you think YOU can run a restaurant?"

"There are too many restaurants ALREADY?"

"You know this will be DIFFICULT to get started?"

Support

All of these responses might be valid. The friend might not have given it enough thought. They might not have experience running a restaurant. There might be a lot of restaurants already. And yes, it will be difficult to start. However, the truth of the matter is, THE PERSON HAS TURNED A DREAM INTO ACTION JUST BY PUTTING IT INTO WORDS! This means that there is a possibility that your friend's dream could become a reality. There is a problem; as a dream stealer you have put up a roadblock!

The dream stealer stops the progress of someone else's dream both with body language and words. At this point, your friend might second guess themselves and wonder if their idea could work. They might rethink their plans and choose a different path because you did not give your approval. This situation plays itself out every time someone asks your opinion about something!

In the African-American community, dream stealers are everywhere! This is because many people do not believe that their dreams can be realized, due to various factors. Lack of education stops some from pursuing their dreams; lack of hope stops others. But the thing that stops people from chasing their dreams the most is OTHER PEOPLE. In other words, the dream stealers in the black community are stopping other African Americans everyday. As a matter of fact, don't be surprised when you find out that some of your family members are dream stealers too!

This is reprehensible! The fact is: some African Americans put up roadblocks for other black people! They steal dreams! It was unfortunate that slave masters stole the dreams of their slaves. It was sad that lawmakers stole the dreams of freed slaves. It was a shame that politicians stole dreams of blacks in the South with segregation. It was a crime that businesses stole the dreams of blacks with workplace discrimination. But above all of this, it is absolutely a tragedy when a black person steals the dreams of another black person!

African Americans have a daunting task of watching out for dream

WAKE UP! 42 Ways to Improve Black America NOW!

stealers in our own community because we all know that negative attitudes seem to be flourishing in our neighborhoods. To do this, we must first identify reasons why one person would want to steal a dream from someone else. Dream stealers come in three categories:

The Miserable One- believes that nothing will work out right. This is probably based on the fact that "nothing" has worked in their lives.

The Advice Giver- believes that their experiences prove that they know good ideas from bad ones. However, there are too many differing factors involved in every experience, so your results will always be different than theirs.

The Evil Doer- believes that it easy easier to sabotage someone else rather than helping them succeed. The evil doer wants you to stay in a state of hopelessness with them.

The best policy is to avoid being one of these three people. Do not be a dream stealer! We can put this into practice by re-examining the restaurant scenario, Instead of asking the questions a dream stealer would use, try the following:

"Let's give this more thought."

"Let's find out how to run a restaurant."

"Let's find an area where there is room for another restaurant."

"This might be difficult to start, but it can be done."

Black America, we need more encouragement, not the theft of dreams. It is hard enough for many of us to overcome daily obstacles on our own. The last thing we need is for our own African- American brothers and sisters to put more obstacles and challenges in our way. The fastest runner must slow down to jump over a hurdle. By being a dream stealer,

Support

you unfairly add extra hurdles to an already lengthy race that we are all running together.

WAKE UP BLACK AMERICA! Don't be a dream stealer!

#39 Give Advice Under Two Conditions

There is an old saying that sheds light on the issue of when, why, and how to give advice. It basically says that most advice is free, but it's not worth the price you pay for it. As African Americans, we should learn how to give support, not give advice. Far too often, we give unwarranted advice based on our viewpoint. In these cases, we should refrain from giving advice, or preface it as an opinion that should not be treated as fact. This way, all of the advice can be properly assessed and considered.

Reality says that there is NO WAY that anyone can be 100% accurate when giving advice. In fact, people who give advice can only offer that advice based on the information they have. Their information is NEVER 100% complete. The only person who has all of the information is YOU! So, you are the only one who can properly assess your needs and therefore, offer yourself the "correct" advice. This also works with someone else. You can not accurately offer advice to someone else because you do not have all of the necessary information. So, we should all be careful with the advice we give to others.

There are two circumstances that warrant giving advice: if you are asked directly for it, and if you are an "expert" in the subject matter! If you can not meet both of these criteria, do not offer your two cents. This is especially true if you want to stick your nose in just for the sake of being nosy. Ask yourself a question: what is my true motivation for giving this advice? Most people will say that they are trying to help. But are they? In their mind, they might be trying to help build something. In reality, they might actually be destroying instead.

An angle that must be looked at is the motivation of the advice giver. Is the advice giver trying to instill fear? Are they trying to prevent or impede your progress? Are they afraid that you can succeed where they could not? Unfortunately, we can only speculate about their true motives. This is why it is important that we are very careful about the advice we ask for, as well as, the people we seek to get advice. The truth is: we are

Support

at the mercy of the advice giver if we are too dependent on what they say.

So many people just give out free advice without being asked for it. In the African-American community, far too often, this advice leads to one conclusion: something can not be accomplished. If you advise another person that it can not be done, are you speaking based on your own assumptions? Absolutely! Perhaps you can not do it, but that doesn't mean they can't. So why "prevent" someone from creating, or at least thinking about, a way to accomplish something. Does this remind you of the dream stealer?

Why do people give advice without asking? It is probably because they pass themselves off as an expert in many different fields. We all know these people: the know-it-alls. They know it all, and they want you to know that they know it all. Therefore, in their mind, they are a jack-of-all-trades. However, we all know about "Jack"; he is a master of none! In other words, Jack does not possess expert knowledge in one given field of expertise. Think about it, would you ask a dentist for advice about fixing a car? Sure, they might know about bicuspids and molars, but do they know brakes and motors?

Experts have a right to offer advice based on their experience. Of course, they must be asked for it first. Experts come in all shapes and sizes in the African-American community, yet many times we choose to follow the wrong ones. For example, the expert drug dealer can give advice on how to sell drugs, but is that advice that will help people improve themselves? On the other hand, the expert black business owner can offer advice on running a business. The question is: why don't we, as African Americans, look to experts in our communities for more advice?

The answer is simple: many of us are afraid to seek out "strangers" who have more "intelligence" than we do! It is frightening to think about a person's reaction when we admit we do not know an answer, or need their help. They might think we are not intelligent enough to figure it out for ourselves. However, in my experience, I have noticed that this is far

WAKE UP! 42 Ways to Improve Black America NOW!

from the truth. Most people who are experts are more than willing to give their advice without any preconceived notions about the person who asks. We just need to seek out these experts.

As a final thought, African Americans can benefit tremendously from the "good" advice of others. In other words, find an expert, ask them for advice, and then apply what you learn to your situation. If you want to open a daycare in the inner city, go into an existing daycare at get some advice. If you want to become a professional athlete, find one and ask for advice. Also, if you are truly an expert, please take the time to help when someone needs advice. Black America can succeed when our advice is given in a supportive way: when it is asked for or when the advice giver is an expert.

WAKE UP BLACK AMERICA! Seek and give advice with care!

Support

#40 Don't Mess With My Code of Ethics

When I was younger, I used to hang out with a crowd of people who like to smoke weed before going out. This was a common thing to do for the so-called benefits smoking marijuana provides. But, I am proud to say that I have never smoked weed, or done any other drug, in my life. As a side note, it absolutely amazes me when people, especially younger ones, ask me if I have ever smoked weed. When they hear my answer, they don't believe me. I guess all young, black men MUST know how to roll a blunt!

How was I able to stay away from the temptation of doing drugs? There was a lot of peer pressure to smoke, pass the joint, or "puff, puff, give", as Chris Tucker said when he played Smokey in the movie *Friday*. At first, I felt strange at those gatherings, especially when the joint made its way to the person next to me. At the moment of truth, when all eyes focused on me, and the weed begged me to take a few hits, I would simple refuse it and let the next person in the circle grab the joint.

The key to the story is what always happened next. No one ever tried to convince me to take that hit. They respected my refusal and moved on. It is true that it meant more for them, but the fact remains: they NEVER pressured me. Soon, this group of people knew not to even ask if I wanted to smoke; they would pass the joint right by me. Even when a newcomer joined the party and didn't know that I wasn't a smoker, they were told immediately to bypass me. The point is: these people respected me enough not to mess with my code of ethics. They respected my desire not to try marijuana.

What is a code of ethics? It is a set of rules or principles that are established as personal guidelines. In this case, my code of ethics was never to experiment with drugs. Everyone has a code of ethics: guidelines on what things they would and would not do in a given situation. The question that plagues many people is how to follow their ethics. Many people are swayed when feeling pressure to break away and follow others regardless of their own belief system.

This represents a huge challenge in the African-American community. I firmly believe African Americans have strong instincts for survival and an unstoppable inner drive to be successful. Our core value system, passed on to us from generation to generation, supports this view, yet we struggle with our ethics on a daily basis. It can be seen on our street corners, where someone came up with the idea of standing on the corner as a way to pass time, sell drugs, or prostitute. If you asked these people if this is the right thing to do, I can guarantee that most would say no.

One of my recurring themes is the concept of acting black vs. acting white. It is a way for some black folks to mess with your code of ethics. Think about it. Why else would someone use this ridiculous concept? For example, who would say that a black person who speaks proper English is acting white? A person who doesn't speak proper English! Obviously, the first person established a rule that learning how to speak properly is necessary. The second person did not. So, it leads me to think saying that an African-American person is acting white is really an attempt to change their belief system.

So how does this occur? It happens because we allow others to influence our decision making. We allow others to lead us, even though we may not want to follow. We blindly go along with the crowd because we fear standing alone. We fear following our belief system. In other words, we allow others to mess with our code of ethics.

The word that best sums up this problem is conformity. Conformity means to go along with something because it is a common thing to do. Sometimes it is good to conform: everyone must go to school to get some form of education. Other times, it is not good to conform: all of my friends are smoking weed so I should smoke too. As black Americans, too many of us seem to overemphasize conforming to destructive behaviors instead of positive ones.

Support

To overcome this, each individual must establish their own code of ethics and constantly work to reinforce them. We should set limits and define boundaries. We should understand what crosses the line. We should identify destructive behaviors that we will never, ever engage in. We should also be aware of others who try to violate these principles and lead us away from our ethics.

African Americans should take heed to this concept. We should let others know our code of ethics whenever the need presents itself. This sends a clear signal that we have boundaries and limits. If we surround ourselves with people who want us to go astray, we will be more likely to abandon our ethics. Therefore, we should not attempt to push others off their moral high ground. Respect the wishes of others, especially when they want to follow their own belief system.

By the way, most of the people I used to hang with are still friends and acquaintances. Although the behavior of smoking weed doesn't happen anymore, if it did and we were in the same old situation, they would still remember not to pass the joint to me. They know not to mess with my code of ethics. It would not be puff, puff, give; it would still be puff, puff, pass!

WAKE UP BLACK AMERICA! Don't try to move me away from my ethics!

WAKE UP! 42 Ways to Improve Black America NOW!

#41 Choose a Positive Role Model

One of the untapped resources of black America is the amount of positive role models we have. Each of these people can, and does, have a profound influence on others. We have numerous examples to choose from, yet many of us fail to choose at all. African-American role models can be found in every city, in all walks of life. A school teacher is a role model. A police officer is a role model. A sanitation worker is a role model. But most importantly, a parent is a role model.

A role model is a person who we model our behavior after. We may or may not know the person, so everyone has the power to be a positive or negative role model. Role models come in all shapes and sizes, colors and creeds, ages and backgrounds. They are people whose behaviors we imitate, even though they may not know it. In fact, many times we are so close to our role models that we do not realize that we are imitating them.

African Americans should be mindful of the fact that SOMEONE IS ALWAYS WATCHING! This is why people can be a positive or negative role model. Friends, who do the right things, can be positive role models. However, if those same friends do the wrong things, they can be negative role models. This is why it is very important to know our children's friends, as well as their families. We must ensure that our children do not fall under negative influences.

EVERYONE IS A ROLE MODEL! Yet our influence can be replaced when we are not around. Therefore, we need to understand that each of us has the power to choose someone to model our behavior after. It is a huge responsibility, yet many African Americans miss out on this golden opportunity. It is important to find a positive male role model for young boys, especially if the father is not around. It is equally important to find a positive role model for young girls, especially if the mother is not around.

Support

Why does black America need positive role models? The answer is simple. We are under attack by negative influences. Everywhere we look, there is tragedy. Everywhere we look, there is heartache. Everywhere we look, there is sorrow. The wonderful news is that there is an equal amount of positive influences that counteract our negative realities, yet many of us fail to see them. For every tragedy, there is a triumph. For every heartache, there is a love story. For every sorrow, there is a spirit of gladness.

We need to counter and conquer negativity before it corrupts another soul. This is why we can not wait any longer. WE MUST STEP UP AND ACCEPT THE CHALLENGE AND RESPONSIBILITY OF BEING POSITIVE ROLE MODELS. Positive role models in the African- American community can deflect negative outcomes in our lives. They can teach us how to handle and overcome our struggles. They can provide a pathway for us to follow. They can open doors that each one of us can enter. We need all of the positive people in the black community to join this struggle.

Where are the positive role models in our communities? They are everywhere! Yet the most powerful role models are in our homes: OUR PARENTS! They are the ones who we model our earliest behaviors after, and most people will exhibit these behaviors for their entire lives. Therefore, I believe the greatest gift a parent can give a child is a POSITIVE OUTLOOK! This can be reinforced correctly when the parent is a positive role model that the child can follow and imitate.

Years ago the great Charles Barkley had a memorable commercial that said he was not a role model. I understood his point, but I believe the writers could have said it better: I should not be your child's most important or only role model. He also said that parents were role models. I understood this as well. He was on target. However, we live in a different world than we had at the time the commercial was made. The situation of black America is improving, but also more perilous now. This is why I applaud him, and all of the pillars of the African American community, who step up and become positive role models.

WAKE UP! 42 Ways to Improve Black America NOW!

Of course, people like Charles Barkley should not be our most important or only role models. This was the main idea of his commercial. Their influence should not take the place of good parents, yet it should be able to provide guidance if parents are not effectively handling their responsibility. An important step to fill the gap of ineffective role models in the home is to have a dialogue about role models in the African American community. WE NEED TO PROMOTE OUR HEROES!

They are everywhere, yet our children do not know them. Our children do not know about black role models and trailblazers because we, as adults, don't know them. Earlier in this book I challenged my readers to get to know some of our greatest citizens. Then, we can teach the information to our children, so that great black Americans can become role models for our children. This is an important, and necessary, step in our journey to improve our communities.

As a final thought, we also have a responsibility not only to our own children, but to all children. You can be a positive role model to a perfect stranger. As stated earlier, SOMEONE IS WATCHING. However, we don't know when they are watching, or what they are looking for. If we demonstrate our goodness, others will emulate it. This is why African Americans MUST learn how to act properly in our homes and in our communities. This sets a great example for others to follow. It is also an outstanding spirit that all positive role models possess and present to others.

WAKE UP BLACK AMERICA! Are you a positive role model?

Support

#42 Surround Yourself With Positive People

If you are a positive person, you will eventually find people who share your good attitude. Remember the law of attraction. Look at the people in your life. Other than family members, think about the overall outlook of your friends and acquaintances. Are they enthusiastic? Once you take inventory, ask yourself a few questions. Do you have more friends who are positive thinkers or negative thinkers? What does this say about you?

Chances are, if you are surrounded by positive people, you are also a positive person. Your relations with these people are going forward in a positive direction. On the other hand, if you are surrounded by negative people, you are a negative person. Your relations with these people are being dragged down in a negative direction. The law of attraction will not have it any other way. In a third scenario, if you have a mix of both positive and negative friends, you will tend to sway back and forth, causing an unhealthy outlook on situations and relationships.

There have been studies that relate health and stress to our mental outlook. Basically, we can improve our health and spirit if we think more positively. We can avoid feeling bad by feeling good! So the obvious conclusion is to find people who share this philosophy. They are a built in support system that everyone needs. All of our African American highest achievers can point to at least one person who was a positive influence on their lives.

Positive people are the anti-dream stealers. They are the dream suppliers! They can influence and motivate, guide and direct, when all else seems to fall apart. For many of us, these people are the teachers who never gave up on us. For others, it might have been a perfect stranger who provided a helping hand in our greatest time of need. People like these are angelic; they are there when we need them. African Americans must find people in their lives that can fill this crucial role.

Another thing that positive people tend to do is not let us lose sight of

WAKE UP! 42 Ways to Improve Black America NOW!

our dreams. They are suppliers who provide the fuel to our fire. They propel us toward greatness and celebrate our success along the way. These positive people are worth their weight in gold! Also, it is even better when these people are experts in their fields and can provide advice based on their own successes.

If you want to be a teacher, find the most positive-thinking teacher you can and seek their advice. This goes for any occupation that you want to hold. Seek out those who can uplift and inspire you to pursue your wildest dreams. Of course, if this person is an African American, then the connection is even stronger for a black person.

Find organizations or groups that are committed to uplifting our race. There you will surely find positive people looking to make positive impacts. These are the people we need to plug in to. They are the leaders of our race. They are the ones who can motivate and inspire other black people to improve their lives. Why? It is because of their positive attitudes and outlooks on their lives that they can help to improve the lives of African Americans worldwide.

The call to action for African Americans is to surround ourselves with positive people. We can learn who they are by listening to the things they say...

Do they share their problems even if not asked to do so, or help others solve problems?

Do they complain a lot or do they actively seek answers to their own problems?

Do they say good or bad things about others?

Do they look for opportunities or claim they do not exist?

Do they strive to be successful or worry about the future?

Support

Think long and hard about the answers to these questions. It will determine the kind of people we surround ourselves with. It also will tell a lot about how we view our circumstances. The only way that African Americans can continue to build our fortunes is by accentuating the positives in our lives. We need people who are proud of their heritage, proud of their culture, and proud of themselves.

Are you a positive person? If not, you should learn how to be more positive. The world is looking for more positive people. African Americans who do not have a positive outlook are ready to follow. Are you ready to lead?

WAKE UP BLACK AMERICA! Surround yourself with positive people!

WAKE UP! 42 Ways to Improve Black America NOW!

The Final Word
❖ ❖ ❖ ❖ ❖ ❖

To everyone who thinks African Americans have made, might make it, or may never make it, here's an analogy for you...

Let's say that you and I are about to have a race. Our race will be continuous. A winner will not be declared until one of us gives up. We will run the same course: a straight line. Good luck, you're going to need it.

There is a catch. I am going to start running before you. In fact, I'll run for 87 hours. 87 refers to years from 1776-1863, you can figure out the dates. At the start of the 88th hour, you can start. When you start, I'll be so far ahead of you that it will take you awhile to catch up: A LONG TIME! When will you be able to catch me? Will it take only 147 hours? (1863-2010) If this is the case, you must be pretty quick!

There's more. Along the way, I have told my friends to put some hurdles in your path. Let's say, there is ONE hurdle to represent the following: the Jim Crow period, the era of segregation, the Civil Rights Era, and post-Civil Rights (discrimination and racial profiling). So, I'll only add FOUR hurdles, but I will make the height of each hurdle different just because I have the power to do so. Do they slow you down?

Finally, ask yourself some questions:

Are you going to quit?
Will you ever ask why the race started the way it did?
Are you ever going to resent the starter, who allowed it to happen?
Will you ever ask for a restart?
Will you get mad, every time you come to another hurdle?
Will you wonder if there are more hurdles you didn't get to yet?
Will you get discouraged, and slow down?

OR...

The Final Word

ARE YOU GOING TO USE WHAT HAPPENED IN THE PAST AS A SPRINGBOARD AND MOTIVATION, AND CONTINUOUSLY RUN AS FAST AS YOU CAN SO THAT ONE DAY, YOU WILL CATCH ME?

Human nature says.....

The point is: I am running fast. Are you running with me? Can you keep pace? Black America, we need to run. We need to keep running. We need to never, ever, under any circumstances, stop running. So I hope to see you on the track. Together, we can catch up and win the race someday.

WAKE UP! 42 Ways to Improve Black America NOW!

About the Author
❖❖❖❖❖❖

Gary A. McAbee is an author and motivational speaker who has developed programs on goal setting and achievement, credit management, and leadership development. He has been involved in education on the secondary and college levels and his teachings have both influenced and impacted many lives. Gary also co-founded ABE! Sports and Entertainment Management in 2000 to meet the needs of professional athletes and artists. He has a Masters Degree in Education from Duquesne University in Pittsburgh and holds numerous certifications and awards.

Gary spent over three years researching and writing because of his desire to help improve the lives of others. As a result, the book WAKE UP! 42 Ways to Improve Black America NOW! became the first volume of his work. His belief is that offering service to others is one of the keys to getting the results that each person strives to attain in life. His philosophy is based on careful study and analysis of some of the highest achievers and most successful people in our history. This knowledge, along with his personal beliefs and experiences, have been blended together to create a self-improvement guide that others can easily use in their daily lives.

"Get Loose and Produce!"

The Final Word

Acknowledgement
❖❖❖❖❖❖

Thank you for completing the first half of the journey with me! In volume two, we will discover 42 more ways that we can use to improve our lives today. I sincerely hope that all people who read this book will apply the principles I have written to achieve outstanding results.

Until we meet again...

Volume Two:

ARE YOU AWAKE YET? 42 Additional Ways to Improve Black America NOW!

WAKE UP! 42 Ways to Improve Black America NOW!

WAKE UP!

Made in the USA
Charleston, SC
29 September 2010